Alex Randall's
USED
COMPUTER
HANDBOOK

Alex Randall's USED COMPUTER HANDBOOK

Dr. Alexander Randall 5th and Steven J. Bennett

PUBLISHED BY
Microsoft Press
A Division of Microsoft Corporation
One Microsoft Way
Redmond, Washington 98052-6399

Library of Congress Cataloging-in-Publication Data

Randall, Alex, 1951–
    Alex Randall's used computer handbook / Alex Randall, S.J.
  Bennett.
       p.   cm.
    ISBN 1-55615-267-1 : $14.95
    1. Used computers — Handbooks, manuals, etc.   I. Bennett, Steven
J., 1951–   .   II. Title.   III. Title: Used computer handbook.
  QA76.5.R34   1990
  004.068'7--dc20   90-5790
                                          CIP

Printed and bound in the United States of America.

1 2 3 4 5 6 7 8 9 RARA 4 3 2 1 0

Distributed to the book trade in Canada by General Publishing Company, Ltd.

Distributed to the book trade outside the United States and Canada by Penguin Books Ltd.

Penguin Books Ltd., Harmondsworth, Middlesex, England
Penguin Books Australia Ltd., Ringwood, Victoria, Australia
Penguin Books N.Z. Ltd., 182-190 Wairau Road, Auckland 10, New Zealand

British Cataloging in Publication Data available

All the events described in this book are based on fact. Some names have been altered
to protect confidentiality. Some incidents are composites of real events related here to
illustrate key points. The views of the authors do not necessarily reflect the views of the
publisher.

Acquisitions Editor: Marjorie Schlaikjer
Project Editor: Erin O'Connor
Technical Editor: Jim Johnson

To Cameron Hall,
without whom there would be no story to tell

CONTENTS

Contents

FOREWORD

by J. Presper Eckert
Coinventor of the ENIAC

A person with a pencil and paper takes about 10 seconds to add two 10-digit numbers. A desk calculator can reduce the time to 4 seconds—about 2.5 times faster. The Harvard Mark I, the last of the electromechanical computers, could add the two 10-digit numbers in 0.3 second—30 times faster than a human with pencil and paper.

The ENIAC, which John Mauchly and I designed and built between 1943 and 1946, was the first electronic digital computer and could add or subtract those numbers in 0.0002 second—50,000 times faster than a human, around 20,000 times faster than a desk calculator, and 1500 times faster than the Harvard Mark I. Scientific calculations, for which the ENIAC could be optimized, ran considerably faster.

An 80286 processor machine, the most common current personal computer, runs about 250,000 operations per second. Depending on the problem, these microprocessors are 25 to 50 times faster than the ENIAC. The personal computer has more than 100 times the memory of the ENIAC, is much more flexible than the ENIAC, and costs less than $\frac{1}{1000}$ of what it would cost to build the ENIAC today.

We frequently calculate computer progress as speed improvement times cost improvement, so we can say that the improvement of the personal computer over the ENIAC is 25 times 1000, or at least 25,000 to 1. The greater memory of the personal computer increases its effective speed and utility even further.

The ENIAC weighed 30 tons, more than 1000 times the weight of today's personal computer. It filled a 30-by-50–foot room and took 150,000 watts to power up. Size and power consumption have thus each been reduced by factors of more than 1000.

The ENIAC blew out one of its 18,000-plus vacuum tubes (radio tubes) every one or two days. With experts running the system, we kept it operating 80 percent, sometimes 90 percent, of the time. A modern personal computer frequently runs for years without a failure. Some recent production hard disk drives are expected to average 100,000 hours before a failure. This comes to more than 4000 days as compared to around a day or so for the ENIAC. Reliability has clearly improved 2000 or 3000 times.

My lowest estimate of the *overall* improvement would be 1 million to 1. It has been 44 years since the ENIAC was born, and about 5 or 6 years since the 80286 came out. This works out to about a 2-to-1 improvement every 2 years, which is a better rate of improvement than that for any technology before in the history of the world!

My goal was to give the world a computer system that was useful, cheap, and reliable. Now personal computers put that goal in everyone's reach. John Mauchly talked to me about a small personal or home computer back in 1955, and we even designed a small magnetic core machine. We couldn't get our sales people to see it as a product back then. Although John Mauchly lived to see only the early home computer revolution, I have been fortunate enough to see almost all the things I used to dream about really happen.

My approach to engineering and my philosophy of computer design have always been to let cost be my guide—specifically the cost of the overall system, not only of certain components. Clearly, this book is in keeping with that philosophy.

The ability to buy good, previously owned personal computers brings systems into the reach of all. The secondary use of computers is probably the only aspect of the computing revolution that John and I did not work on. That's why I am so pleased not only to write this foreword to *Alex Randall's Used Computer Handbook*, but also to recommend strongly that you acquire and read this book. Buying a good used computer system is one way to get the highest possible performance for an affordable price, and this book should help you do so.

Gladwyn, Pennsylvania
January 1990

PREFACE

We originally tried to sell this book to a major trade publisher. The idea didn't fly because the editor-in-chief, still stuck in the typewriter era, didn't understand why people might trade PCs. "After all," she said, "people don't buy used televisions, so why would they want to buy used computers? No deal."

This misconception illustrates an important point—computers are not like TVs. Or like VCRs. Or like any other electronic goods. Computers are different because the underlying technology evolves almost daily. Even though PCs last for ten years or more, at the cutting edge they become obsolete in as little as six months. But despite ongoing advances in memory, speed, and overall capability, any PC in working order, regardless of vintage, can be put to good use by someone. One person's antique computer is always another's technological windfall.

Why? Because computers are thinking tools above all else. They help people reduce tedium and escape drudgery, and they amplify the capabilities of the human mind. Everything that got us excited about PCs more than a decade ago is still true today; the front edge has moved on, but the revolution continues.

We are deeply grateful to the people at Microsoft Press for understanding the mission of computers in our modern world and for having the courage to gamble on a book that's somewhat off the beaten path.

Very special thanks go to Acquisitions Editor Marjorie Schlaikjer for sharing our vision and helping us to shape a book that we hope will someday put a PC on every desk. We're also indebted to Director of Marketing and Acquisitions Jim Brown, General Manager Patty Stonesifer, Senior Acquisitions Editor Dean Holmes, and Publicist Craig Johnson for supporting our project.

For supporting our collective "voice," we'd like to thank our manuscript editor Erin O'Connor, who gasped and proceeded to scrap the house stylebook. She and principal proofreaders Cynthia Riskin and Kathleen Atkins fell in with our intentions and permitted us most of our excesses.

We thank our agent Michael Snell for cluing us in to the needs of normal, low-tech human beings and Wyon Budi Utamo and Padi Dell of Ubud, Bali, for planting the seeds of this book.

Technical Editor Karl Koessel of *PC World* reviewed early drafts of the manuscript for technical accuracy and pointed out our biases and misunderstandings. We're grateful to Karl and to Jim Johnson, who reviewed later drafts. If mistakes remain, they are our own.

We'd also like to express our thanks to Dr. Alexander Randall IV and Dr. Nina Perlingiero Randall, who took their son Alex to see a UNIVAC when he was a child. Transfixed by the lights, switches, and dials, Alex became a computer junkie before he could read.

Alex's former teacher Margaret Mead was an inspiration for this book. Margaret had the foresight in 1973 to convince Alex of the worthiness of investigating how societies consume new technology and the stumbling blocks that keep a new technology from being adopted. Had it not been for that research project, Alex would never have understood the importance of processing the trailing edge of a new technology.

This book would never have happened without the support of our families. We thank our wives, Cameron Hall (Randall) and Ruth Loetterle (Bennett), for doing double duty at the diaper changing tables while we did triple duty at our keyboards. We are most grateful to our infant sons, Alexander Randall VI and Noah Andrew Bennett, for saving us places in their playrooms. Thanks, guys—we'll make it up to you in good software.

INTRODUCTION

Ubud, Bali, is a low-tech town. Women wash their clothes in the river and cook on open fires. Village men sow rice by hand, knee deep in the lush paddies. Even so, in this remote, primitive corner of the world I saw my first personal computer. Like the 1000-year-old irrigation system terraced into the mountainside, the PC was appropriate technology for the time and place—housed in a wooden crate and powered by a refurbished exercise bike connected to an old truck generator.

The brainchild of UNESCO food scientist Sean Foley, this 8KB powerhouse was the key to survival for thousands of people in the Third World. Sean put the system together to determine whether IR-36 was really the "miracle rice" of the Green Revolution so many agronomists claimed it was. Even though IR-36 yielded more rice on the same amount of land than conventional strains and could be harvested in 90 instead of 210 days, Sean suspected that the real costs of the new hybrid might be high. Did the extra human labor, duck guano, and urea fertilizer offset the benefits of the faster, higher yield?

The answer to the question of how much energy went in and how much food came out required numerous iterations of complex equations that would have taken weeks to perform on a hand calculator. Sean assembled the home-brewed computer from scratch, and for weeks pedaled away on the exercise bike as he keyed in data.

Watching that primitive PC solve a complicated science problem was mind-boggling. Sean's ingenious, bicycle-powered contraption was actually figuring out how best to use land to feed people. It could make the difference between hungry or healthy children, even the difference between life and death. I asked myself, "How many millions of people can I help feed if I get this guy a real computer, and how can I get better computer technology into the hands of other people who will make a real difference?"

FROM DUCK GUANO IN BALI TO DATABASES IN BOSTON

A month later I found myself at Princeton University giving a talk about computers and social change at my alma mater's School of Engineering. I talked about Sean and the impact of his computer on Balinese agriculture and about creating a better world through computing. I talked about linking people through personal computers and the coming age of the global electronic village.

On the drive back home to Boston, these thoughts stayed with me, and an idea began to take shape. It seemed so good that I pulled over and called my wife, Cameron Hall. The gist was that we'd find people who'd outgrown their computers and introduce them to people who could be way ahead with someone else's old technology. If we could do that, I said to Cameron, we could accelerate the flow of computer technology. We'd recycle—update people's systems and help people get rid of their old systems. We'd make a difference—improve people's minds and the whole world. From a business standpoint, we'd act as brokers, taking a modest commission for connecting those who have with those in need.

Cameron jumped on the idea. By the time I got home she'd already written up a flier to take to a meeting of the newly formed Boston Computer Society Osborne User's Group. We passed out our flier along with blue index cards for buyers and orange cards for sellers, asking people to fill them out and mail them back to us.

Within two days we had more than 500 potential buyers and sellers, and as calls came in we spread out the cards on our living room floor. We made matches from our "flatfile database," called the parties, and helped them trade systems.

Nearly a decade later, Cameron and I sit in the executive suite of the Boston Computer Exchange Building, overlooking Boston's historic Downtown Crossing. In a typical day, a platoon of brokers manage more than 1000 phone calls while their computers search the database and update it with the latest entries. At the end of each day, the state of the market is transmitted to four on-line electronic services, and each Friday afternoon, the week's bid, ask, and closing prices for the most popular models are beamed to newspapers and magazines throughout the world—even to Bali.

THE SECONDARY COMPUTER MARKET

Why did the idea for the Boston Computer Exchange catch on? Because of situations like these, with their splendid opportunities for matchmaking, which happen every day:

- You finally decide to buy a word processor to write the novel that's been floating around in your head for the past 10 years. You go to a computer store and decide to let the great work gestate a bit longer after you learn you could spend $5,000 to buy a new computer.

- Your old dual floppy disk drive computer can't run the new generation of high powered desktop publishing software. You can't afford to buy a new, more powerful computer until you get some cash for the old PC. After weeks of trying to sell your machine through want ads and the local church gazette, you haven't had any takers. The trade-in amount dealers offer won't even pay for the electricity to run a new computer. How do you find a buyer for your old computer?

- Your small company is rapidly outgrowing your basement, but it still isn't stable enough to support additional overhead and capital expenditures. Your five employees fight for their turns at the company's 1980 TRS-80 computer, still huffing away on its single floppy disk drive accounting program. Somehow, you must provide your people with the technology they need to do their jobs without making a major financial commitment you might not be able to meet.

■ Your boss has just slashed your marketing department's capital equipment budget by 25 percent. At the same time, an economy move to bring such work in-house has placed the responsibility for a series of product promotion campaigns squarely on your shoulders. You determine that your existing equipment won't do the job and that you will need at least five high-performance computers and at least three state-of-the-art laser printers. You've considered some low-end mail order "clones," but your technical advisers have questioned their service records. Somehow, you must buy higher quality hardware for less money and get rid of a whole department's worth of computers and printers you can't use anymore.

These are but a few of the scenarios we hear about through our brokers and customers, and one person's problem is often another person's solution. More people want computers for personal use than ever before. And more companies are running up against the need to contain runaway capital equipment costs without hampering productivity or losing competitiveness. At the same time, individuals and companies have older PCs they want to sell. They find themselves stuck with obsolete equipment as the pace of computer technology shortens product life spans.

The answer to all these problems lies in the "secondary computer market," a jungle of perfectly good equipment ready to solve many of the most demanding computing problems at bargain prices. For the uninitiated buyer, though, it's no easy task to grope through the options for locating used computer equipment—newspaper want ads, trade-ins, liquidations, swap meets, consignment stores, donations, and hand-me-downs, to name a few. For the seller, it's no easier. What's it worth? Who's going to buy it?

A GUIDE FOR THE PERPLEXED

The good news is that buying and selling used computer equipment can be a win-win proposition in which the buyer and the seller both come out ahead. Finding the equipment you need at the right price can be a simple and pleasurable exercise—if you know what you want and where to look. Selling your existing machine might take no more than a phone call—if you know where to call.

This book will arm you with the information you need to become a savvy trader in the computer marketplace. It will help you get the most used computer for your money and the most money for your used computer. I won't have to mention many brand names in the following pages because I'll teach you generic principles for buying and selling used machines. These principles, based on a decade's experience in the secondary market, will work in 1990 and in the year 2000. They're really about personal needs assessment and product life spans. By teaching you these principles, I hope to provide you with tools for understanding cycles of change so that you'll know when to buy and when to sell. I'll teach you the language of the market so that you can talk to traders in any time and place.

Beyond the mechanics of trading in the marketplace, this book will teach you how to recycle your computer and become a responsible, ecological consumer of technology. The world already has more than enough technology to go around, and as new generations of computers and chips are introduced, you can redistribute your outgrown gear to people who really need it and are ready to grow into it.

Finally, by recycling your old technology, whether it goes to a volunteer in the rice paddies or a start-up entrepreneur, you help empower the whole world. By updating your computer system and sending your old gear down the line, you help everyone work faster and smarter. My teacher and friend Margaret Mead (who sent me to Bali) once told me to "think of the whole planet at once, and eliminate the bottlenecks in the flow of new ideas." I tried to do that in Boston when Cameron and I launched the Computer Exchange. I do it today as I figure out how to get more computers into the hands of people who need them.

Whether you need a computer to calculate the bottom line for your business or the amount of duck guano per bag of rice, I urge you to buy a machine with a past. When you outgrow it, sell it and move on to the next level. You'll promote the health of your checkbook and get the right computer for your task. That's what appropriate technology is about.

Alexander Randall 5th
Boston, Massachusetts
January 1990

CHAPTER 1

TIMELESS TECHNOLOGY

Selling and Buying Your Way into the Next Generation

❧

Randall's Notebook

December 3, 1980

Akihabara, Tokyo

❧

If it's electronic, you can find it here. And cheap. It's a bizarre bazaar. Vendors display their wares in little rabbit hutch rooms packed side-by-side, but instead of fabrics, foodstuffs, and handcrafts, these people sell everything from stereos and camcorders to chips and dip switches. Each vendor specializes in an item. One hutch features televisions and another's focus is processor chips. One hutch has RAM chips and another video gear.

I rummage through a shop chock-full of calculators and pick up a curious model. The right side has push buttons and an LCD display—it's clearly a calculator. The left side appears to be a miniature abacus.

"Is this some kind of gag item?" I ask the proprietor.

He puts his hands to his throat as he struggles to understand my question. Realizing his confusion, I rephrase the question. He finally answers, in broken English, "No, this for real use."

"Why would you need an abacus if you have a calculator?" I ask incredulously.

Shocked by my ignorance, he replies, "Have to make sure calculator is right."

◆➤

REVENGE OF THE ABACUS

Great technology is never obsolete because obsolescence is in the eyes of the user. To a Westerner, the abacus seems as primitive as stone knives and spears. But if you do an abacus level of math, its performance suits your needs. Consider the groundbreaking machines of the computer era. The ENIAC, the world's first real electronic digital computer, weighed 30 tons and occupied 1500 square feet. Its 18,000 vacuum tubes and 70,000 resistors soaked up 150,000 watts of electricity every time the machine was powered up. To "program" the machine (to calculate artillery trajectory tables for the war effort) took hours of work with 5000 manual switches and several hundred wire patch panels. Nevertheless, it did what it was supposed to do. Sure, by today's standards the ENIAC was painstakingly slow, but it enabled people to solve problems that would have been even more tedious and impossibly slow to solve by hand.

The ENIAC's successor, the UNIVAC, did nifty tricks such as predicting that Dwight Eisenhower would win the 1952 presidential election. The UNIVAC also did serious analytical tricks—helping the US Census Bureau analyze who's who in America, for instance. The UNIVAC also helped companies (General Electric was one) cut paychecks and track their accounts payable. If you could find a UNIVAC and someone who knew how to run it today, you could still use it to analyze the census or run a company's accounting department. Almost any personal computer would do the job faster and in a fraction of the space at a fraction of the cost, but if you had the time, the space, and a suitable application, the principles underlying the UNIVAC's technology wouldn't be obsolete.

Computer technology is appropriate as long as it does the job. This is a radical concept, given all the hype in the computer industry. We see legitimate advances in chip design and computer architecture that let us do things with desktop computers that were unheard of in the early 1980s when the personal computer revolution was in its infancy. But the pace of the technology seems to increase weekly. The jump from the original PC chips to the second generation chips took more than three years. The subsequent generation appeared in less than one year. The third generation was well on its way to becoming obsolete only a year after it was state of the art. By the time you read this book, who knows what generation of chip will be the latest and greatest? No other technology in human history has progressed as quickly as this one.

The pressure of this pace calls for a realistic assessment of your needs against the current state of the art. You need to judge what hardware and software are appropriate for your computing tasks.

THE TECHNOLOGICAL CONTINUUM

A technology can be graphed on a continuum of possibilities, with the simplest forms at one end and the most complex at the other—from quill pens at one end to computers equipped with supercooled parallel processors at the other. As we'll see shortly, the most sophisticated technology at the complex end of the continuum is not necessarily "better" than a simpler technology farther back. It's all a matter of what's appropriate for you.

Suppose, for example, that you want to get from point A to point B. Do you need a car, a motorcycle, or a bicycle, or would a pair of roller skates get you there? If point B is only a few blocks away, human locomotion might be most appropriate. If you do need a car, will a vintage VW Beetle do, or do you need a Jaguar XJ6? Are you taking cargo? Do you need a one-ton truck or an 18-wheeler? Is it too far to drive? Perhaps you should fly. Will a Piper Cub suffice, or do you need a Lear Jet? Do you need a Boeing 747, or will it take the Concorde to do the job?

Now suppose that you want to send a message to someone in another city. If several days from now is soon enough, you'll use the regular postal service. If you have to get it there tomorrow, you'll use an overnight delivery service. If you have to plop the piece of paper on the other person's desk within seconds, you'll use either a FAX machine or a modem. There are always occasions for primitive technology. (No, Mr. Morse, we don't need your telegraph machine— these carrier pigeons do the job just fine.) And occasions for which the state of the art is not enough. (Special Relativity Express— when you absolutely, positively have to have it there yesterday.)

The same, of course, applies to writing, counting, cataloging, and other information-based tasks. You can write a letter with a quill pen and count your change with an abacus, or you can write a letter on a $100,000 dedicated page composition system and count your change with a $17 million Cray supercomputer. Using either the dedicated system or the supercomputer, of course, would be like launching the space shuttle to go to the corner store. You need some index of appropriate fit. You determine that fit by examining your needs, which are defined by two basic questions: What do I need today, and what do I need tomorrow? Let's deal with today first.

SCENARIOS FOR THE HERE AND NOW

For a computer system to be of use to you, you must understand its capabilities and your requirements. For example, on an arbitrary scale of 1 to 10, a dual floppy drive computer might register 1 in terms of what it can do, and the current state-of-the-art hard disk system might register 10. But if all you're doing is writing simple, one-page letters, both systems might register 10 in terms of what they can do for you. The significant difference to you is that you'd spend a few hundred dollars for a used dual floppy drive machine but many thousands of dollars for a spanking-new speed demon fresh out of the laboratory.

Rather than ask about megabytes of memory, megahertz of speed, or megapixels of display, you'd do well to ask yourself a few questions.

1. What do I need to do?
2. What configuration will do it?
3. What can I afford?

Let's analyze the first two questions from the standpoint of the most common tasks people do with computers. For each job that has to be done, you'll find a low-end, a mid-level, and a high-end technology. These are rough divisions. For our purposes, the low end refers to systems only a notch above their manual counterparts. The mid-level refers to computers that reviewers call "workhorses." They won't break any speed records but will dependably run most mainstream software. The high end refers to cutting edge devices that have just made the headlines. To help you figure out what you need, we'll look at the most common computing tasks in terms of roughly three levels of jobs and at the technology that will do the jobs from the low end through the high end. Note that throughout this book, you'll be encouraged to evaluate your needs and the market in generic terms rather than in terms of specific machine models.

Word Processing

Low end. You use your computer to write letters and memos. You can get by with a dual floppy drive system, a monochrome text monitor, and a dot matrix or daisy wheel printer. Any simple word processor will do—you don't need to spend money or learning time on a full-featured professional program. You might even use a Shareware or public domain word processing program or one bundled with the computer.

Mid-level. You type 300-page manuscripts and must integrate text and graphics. You need a workhorse computer with a hard disk and a good resolution black-and-white monitor capable of graphics although not necessarily a state-of-the-art system. The performance of most word processing functions, with the exception of spell checking, improves only marginally with increased power.

You'll definitely want a laser printer. You'll also want a full-featured word processor.

High end. You type complex technical documents in multiple languages. Your work frequently calls for special fonts as well as a variety of type styles. You integrate scientific charts, graphs, and illustrations into your text, and the text must flow around them. You must be able to see on the screen what the finished pages will look like when they pop out of the printer. You need an industrial strength system—a computer with a first class, high resolution black-and-white or color monitor and the latest laser printer. A top-tier word processor with special add-ins will be in order.

Desktop Publishing

Low end. You create simple fliers and announcements, restaurant menus, or posters. You need a mid-performance hard disk machine, a black-and-white graphics monitor, and a laser printer. An entry-level desktop publishing program will do, but you might outgrow it very quickly.

Mid-level. You do page composition to create sophisticated brochures, manuals, and newsletters. You need the most powerful computer, the highest resolution monitor, and a laser printer. Be prepared to buy a more functional desktop publishing program—you'll need it and use it to the maximum.

High end. You handle the company's annual report, newsletters for the stockholders, and formal presentations. You not only do page composition, but you also create charts and graphs and scan photographs and integrate them into text. You need an "artstation" with horsepower on all fronts: a fast processor and a big, fast hard disk. Because so much of your work is "processor intensive," no matter what chip is currently state of the art, you'll jump to the next level as soon as it's available—they haven't got a PC that's fast enough for you. The same holds for high resolution monitors—"pixel madness" will steadily drain your bank account, as will the introduction of ever-higher resolution printers and scanners and live-action presentation devices. You'll want professional typesetting equipment and a professional-level desktop publishing program.

Graphics/Drawing

Low end. You create simple business graphs and simple free-form art. A first generation processor with dual floppies and a graphics display card and graphics monitor will be enough to get you going. You need an ink jet or a dot matrix printer. An entry-level graphics program from the public domain will cover the task.

Mid-level. You produce presentation quality business or scientific graphics or design sophisticated artwork or logos. All graphics tasks call for a high-performance computer, a big, fast hard disk, and a high resolution monitor. You need a laser printer or a plotter. At this level you'll want a mainstream professional graphics program.

High end. You do computer aided design (CAD) or computer aided engineering (CAE). You need a graphics workstation, and now you're talking real state-of-the-art equipment—the faster and more powerful, the better. You need the highest resolution monitor, a laser printer, and possibly even a jumbo floor-standing plotter big enough to sleep three. The system unit should include the latest and fastest processor with matching math coprocessor. You'll want sophisticated, professional software capable of three-dimensional work. No matter what you have, you're always in the market for something even more powerful.

Communications

Low end. You "conference" with other people on Compu-Serve, make travel arrangements with Official Airline Guide, and send an occasional file to a colleague. All you need is a dual floppy drive machine with a basic modem. A basic communications program, one that simply lets you send and receive files, will do.

Mid-level. You send your daily column to your editors in New York, Boston, and San Jose. You beam an occasional article to a friend or another editor elsewhere in the country. A computer with a fast processor and a hard disk will speed things up. So will a high-level modem. The communications program you buy should offer some degree of programmability although a basic send-and-receive-files package will probably be adequate.

High end. You integrate files from branch offices around the world. This is strictly a state-of-the-art endeavor. You need the fastest high-end telecommunication devices available—an internal FAX board, a communications coprocessor, or more. You'll probably want a communications package that contains a "command language" so that you can write your own automated calling "scripts" for firing off reports to multiple target locations through the night while you take in raw data from the daylight centers on the flip side of the planet.

Spreadsheets

Low end. You're in the family budget league, which means you balance your checkbook and do an occasional mortgage comparison. You can make do with a dual drive system, a cheap dot matrix printer, and software that can run without a hard disk.

Mid-level. You do basic bookkeeping and figure out the annual budget for a small business, or you track a stock portfolio. You need a "workhorse" computer with a graphics monitor and a high quality dot matrix printer—probably with a wide carriage. You might even want to spring for a laser printer. You'll want a mainstream spreadsheet package.

High end. You've graduated to three-dimensional spreadsheet computing. You've left line graphs and bar charts behind and show your numbers in stacked symbols in three dimensions. You do sophisticated modeling and analysis and want to print your reports in professional, presentation quality formats, including 35mm color slides. You need a high horsepower processor with a math coprocessor, a large, fast hard disk, a high resolution monitor, a laser printer, possibly a color plotter, and other presentation facilities such as a slide maker or projection video.

Database Management

Low end. You manage a Christmas card mailing list or a batch of recipes. A dual drive system might suffice, along with a dot matrix printer. For mailing labels, you might want a used daisy wheel printer. A simple "flat file" database package, commercial or public domain, will probably do the job just fine.

Mid-level. You want to automate your small business inventory system. You're going to need a hard disk system, a decent resolution monitor, and probably a printer capable of producing fairly condensed print. The printer model will depend on aesthetics—you might want a laser printer if customers need to read your output. Rather than buy a canned software package that might not suit your special needs, hire a database programmer to design and write a custom invoicing program.

High end. Your team manages a 25,000-name mailing list or generates on-hand inventory balances for thousands of parts in a warehouse. You need state-of-the art horsepower and a very large capacity, very fast hard disk. Any monitor with reasonable resolution will do. You'll want real custom programming or a dedicated database package.

These scenarios are but a few of the situations people find themselves in when they have to assess their computing needs. You get the idea, though, and should be able to get a gross notion of where your needs fall on the technological continuum. The next step is to think about your future needs.

TOMORROW

"Buy more than you need—you'll grow into it." Planning ahead that way can put a company out of business. Think about how many companies go belly-up before they use the resources they overbought either to get a price break or to anticipate the future. We tend to overbuy on the assumption that it's better to commit resources now than to get caught with our pants down later. This mentality can kill a business.

The same mentality can waste your valuable computing dollars. Let's say that your current computing needs are low end but that you expect to do mid-level jobs within a year and a half and high-end computing jobs in about two years.

If you go out and buy the top-of-the-line, state-of-the-art system, you will surely pay a premium price—in all likelihood, you won't find a used state-of-the-art system, and the manufacturer won't drop the price until it's ready to release a new high-end model. (See Chapter 3 for a discussion of pricing curves.) Worst of all, the darned thing probably won't even be debugged when you get it—you'll be just another beta test site. And given the pace of technological change, by the time you'll be ready for that high-end computing you anticipated, your computer will be anything but state of the art. You'll be ready for the next step and already out of step! This might happen even by the time you reach mid-level computing tasks. You'll have paid top dollar for a machine that might not run current software as well as current computers do—or for a machine that might not be able to run the current software at all.

One of the saddest stories from the annals of the Boston Computer Exchange concerns an architect who needed a computer to conduct a lighting study. He knew he could buy a minimum power Apple to do the job, but he foresaw bigger and more complex projects he could take on if he had more computing power down the road, and there was talk of new software in the works for the next level of Apple machines. Instead of buying the configuration that would handle the task at hand, he bought the most advanced Apple system of the day—the Lisa 10. Thirty-six hours later, Apple announced that it was dropping the whole Lisa line in favor of their new Macintosh computers. Lisa became an orphan.

There's a lesson to be learned from this sad Lisa story; nevertheless, you should consider your future computing needs and ask yourself the following questions:

1. What's the next stage of growth for me?
2. What's the next level of hardware and software beyond the minimum system I need right now?
3. How far can I stretch my budget?
4. What's the next stage of growth for the industry?

"Now wait a minute," you're probably thinking, "a page ago you jokers told me *not* to worry about buying for the future." The real problem, of course, is buying *too* far ahead rather than only a "little bit" ahead. If all you want to do is write letters, you could conceivably get by with an electronic typewriter. But think ahead to the day you might want to type long manuscripts. If there's even a remote possibility that you will, it makes sense to spring for the next-level configuration that's still within your budget—a dual floppy drive machine or even an inexpensive hard disk–based machine.

Unless you're certain that you're in a no-growth situation, an entry-level system will be a poor value. The slightly higher cost of buying additional power is negligible compared to the utility that more computer power provides. Regardless of the system you buy, a fair portion of the price will be accounted for by the "box" and basic guts, which are the same for many models.

At the very least, be sure that the system you buy is minimally expandable. In the next chapter, we'll look at upgrades, another path to higher levels of computing.

SELLING DOWN, BUYING UP

The good news for everybody is that no matter where your needs fall on the technological spectrum, the secondary computer market offers you tremendous mobility. What the guy at the low end outgrows might be exactly what the little guy needs to get started in home computing. The techno wizard at the high end might find the mid-level person a willing and eager recipient of his or her once state-of-the-art hardware. The high-end techno wizard can take the cash and buy that new machine as it rolls out of the laboratory.

Computers actually hit the secondary market surprisingly quickly. Sometimes it's only a matter of a few months before recently introduced equipment lands in the Boston Computer Exchange database. Table 1-1 shows how little time it has taken some models to reach the used market.

Brand	Model	Date of introduction	Date of first used listing
Apple	Mac Plus	January 1986	May 1986
Apple	Mac SE	March 1987	August 1987
Apple	Mac SE/20	March 1987	January 1988
Compaq	386	September 1986	August 1987
Toshiba	T-3100	November 1986	December 1986
IBM	XT	March 1983	March 1985
IBM	AT	August 1984	April 1985
IBM	PS/2 30	April 1987	January 1988
IBM	PS/2 80	April 1987	January 1988
IBM	PS/2 50Z	April 1988	February 1989

Table 1-1.
Introduction date and date of first appearance in the
secondary market for some major models.

IBM AND COMPATIBLES

Models	PC → XT → AT → PS/2
Processors	8086 → 8088 → 80186 → 80286 → 80386 → 80486
Memory	16KB → 64KB → 256KB → 512KB → 640KB → 1MB
Monitors	Monochrome → Hercules Graphics → CGA → EGA → VGA → SuperVGA → 8514A
Mass Storage	Floppy Disks: 320KB → 360KB → 1.2MB → 720KB → 1.44MB Hard Drives: 10MB → 20MB → 30, 40 . . . 300MB. . .

APPLE II

Models	I → II → II+ → IIe → IIc → IIgs

All Apple II models, with the exception of the IIgs, contain 6502 processors and 143K floppy disk drives. The differences in models lie primarily in keyboards and monitors.

MACINTOSH

Models	128 → 512 → 512e → Plus → SE → Mac II → Mac IIx → SE/30 → Mac IIcx → Mac IIci → Mac IIfx
Processors	68000 → 68020 → 68030 → 68040
Monitors	Monochrome → Variety of high resolution models, monochrome and color
Mass Storage	Floppy Disks: 400K → 800K → Super1.4M Hard Drives: 5M → 10M → 20M → 40M → 80M

This mobility has been a characteristic of the electronic computer age. Consider the journey of UNIVAC 1, the first computer to become a commercial success. After the Bureau of the Census outgrew their UNIVAC's capacity, the machines were sold down the line to other owners until one UNIVAC wound up in the Smithsonian Institution as a tribute to Yankee ingenuity. Meanwhile, the Bureau has continually traded up, so that today it still does business with the top of the line—the Unisys mainframe, a direct descendent of UNIVAC 1. The Bureau of the Census incidentally set precedents for a secondary technology market in which users sell down and buy up as their needs change.

Today, personal computers travel the same path. The cycling and recycling of PC technology is well-illustrated by a history of the tools that have managed data at the Boston Computer Exchange. The Exchange's database started at the absolute low end of the technological continuum with a "dual pile index card" system, complete with ballpoint pen. It then expanded into a dual floppy drive system. When the database grew too big for a single floppy disk, it moved into a machine with a 10-megabyte hard disk. That machine sprouted a terminal so that two people could work at the same time. When sluggish speed became a problem, the database moved into an IBM AT. Subsequent generations of data management have led to local area networks, relational databases, and massive file servers. The original dual floppy drive PC that powered the Exchange has been traded at least a dozen times and is currently helping someone else get his business rolling.

The chart on the opposite page shows you how the main lines of personal computers—the IBM PC and compatibles, the Apple II, and the Macintosh—have evolved.

As you consider whether you'll buy or sell a used computer, refer to the chart so that you'll know where the machine in question fits into the general scheme of things.

Randall's Rules

- ➡ One person's throwaway is another's gold.
- ➡ When your tools limit you, it's time to replace them.
- ➡ Buy as much as you need and a little more for growth.

CHAPTER 2

FIVE-MINUTE MICRO MAKEOVERS

Upgrading Your PC vs. Selling It

➼

Randall's Notebook

January 3, 1989

Boston, Massachusetts

➼

Cameron and I groan—the racket in the hallway of the Exchange building can mean only one thing, a seller with a shopping cart. What hodgepodge of mismatched, abused, and obsolete computer junk bounces along inside? Computers hot off the shelf—really hot? A seaweed-stained DEC Rainbow last used to analyze the copulation rate of turtles in the Galapagos Islands? A hole-ridden Osborne I that's survived a barrage of Sandinistan antiaircraft flak?

We've seen it all. Or so we think. The cart finally emerges, along with its power train—a bespectacled, gangly man in his late thirties. He started out with a 16KB IBM PC with the cassette tape drive. The box he walks in with, though, sports an outrageous assortment of add-in boards, enhancement products, and extension extenders; it's the

17

digital equivalent of the "octopus plug." The shopping cart contains three or four generations of add-in and add-on boards and accessories, including the original motherboard and an upgrade motherboard, two generations of disk drives, and four generations of monitors and adapter cards. He finally "hit the wall" when he discovered that his Rube Goldberg computer wouldn't run OS/2, and now he's decided to bite the bullet and buy a new high-end machine. Figuring he'll cash in with his cartful of goodies first, he proudly announces that he paid $14,000 for all the junk in his cart and is willing to accept 10 percent less than his original investment.

We offer him $900—a generous offer—at which point he and his shopping cart storm out the door.

Later, when we leave the Exchange to walk home, we see a trail of computer parts. "Ashes to ashes, silicon to silicon," I say to Cameron. She nods and we head for the Boston Common, pondering whether good technologies have good karma and return for another round of life.

➼

UPGRADE MANIA SYNDROME

IBM designed the original PC to be a general purpose system that could be expanded. That's what those "slots" on the back of the computer are all about. Actually, they're not on the back; they're on the computer's "bus," the interstate highway that connects everything to the computer's brain, or central processing unit (CPU).

Interestingly, despite the seeming complexity of the PC, the entire apparatus is much like a set of Tinker Toys or Legos housed in a metal box. Almost everything snaps in, pulls out, or unplugs and reassembles, so that you need only a screwdriver and some intestinal fortitude to disassemble and renovate a PC. Even the least technical user with a little bit of initiative and a small sack of cash can upgrade a computer in a matter of minutes.

So why not simply upgrade instead of buying a whole new machine? Often, upgrading does make sense and can be a great way to stretch the utility of your machine for less money than a new one would cost. But upgrading has definite limits, after which you'll throw money into a machine that will never deliver the functionality of a later generation computer and that will acquire only a slight premium on its resale value. When people go past the upgrade limits, they're probably driven by Upgrade Mania Syndrome (UMS) and aren't responsible for their actions.

UMS creeps up on its victim slowly, beginning with an innocuous, modest investment to improve performance. One RAM board begets a daughter board, which begets a hard disk that demands a new power supply. The additional power begets a PostScript interpreter board, and so on, until the power supply has a whole family of hungry new components to feed. And the victim wakes up in a cold sweat one day, realizing he's sunk more money into the old PC than it would cost to buy a new one. As one customer of the Exchange put it, "Once you get started, it's like losing a clotting factor in your checkbook."

In this chapter you'll find rules of thumb for making intelligent decisions about when to upgrade and when to sell. In the first part, you'll learn what upgrades make sense and how to evaluate their hidden costs. In the second, you'll examine the worst effects of UMS—what happens when you go overboard with your add-in board, embark on a rabid RAM-board rampage, or get lost in megadisk hyperspace.

SENSIBLE UPGRADE PATHS

Ideally, a computer system is a collection of components matched in their levels of performance. For any component, potential replacements range from just a little more powerful to outrageously more powerful. A component that's outrageously more powerful than the rest of the components is a waste of money, like adding a fireproof metal door to a wood-frame house.

Let's say that you have an early generation Macintosh system and want to add a hard disk. You could spring for a relatively inexpensive, relatively slow hard disk or pay top dollar for a state-of-the-art, greased lightning unit. Regardless of which disk you bought, keyboard command response time would be about the same because the speed of the processor would be a bottleneck. In this case, spending more money for faster access time won't appreciably improve performance because the high-speed disk will be held back by the relatively slow performance of the components under the Macintosh hood.

As a rule, don't replace a single component with a component that exceeds the performance level of the other components in the system.

GOOD UPGRADES AND THEIR HIDDEN COSTS

As you try to make sensible upgrade choices, be aware of the hidden costs. It's never as simple as it seems.

Hard Disk Drives

The transition from floppy disk to hard disk is like losing your virginity—you can never go back. Hard disks are that much faster and more convenient than floppies. After working with a hard disk for about four seconds, you'll find floppies intolerably slow. And hard disks are much less prone to damage and data loss. A dirty fingerprint on a floppy disk can mean the end of your data, as can any other manhandling. Finally, when you have a hard disk, you can use the thousands of software packages that don't run on floppy systems.

In the old days, only corporations and dedicated hackers bought hard disks. Today, prices are down and performance is up. IBM's first external hard disk for the PC listed at more than $3,000 and held an awesome 10 megabytes of data—about twenty-eight 5.25-inch floppy disks' worth. Despite the more than $300 per megabyte price and access times measured in macroseconds, the computer magazine pundits suggested that by strapping one of those babies onto your dual drive PC you'd create a veritable "fire-breather."

At the beginning of 1990, a good 40-megabyte hard disk lists at about $450 ($11 per megabyte) and costs as little as $290 used ($7 per megabyte). And 60-megabyte, 120-megabyte, and 330-megabyte disks are common, with cost-per-megabyte approaching $5. The original price of the IBM 10-megabyte hard disk would buy 800 megabytes of storage today—an 80-fold increase. The price of storage is falling dramatically.

The old 10-megabyte clunker operated at 85 milliseconds, making it painfully slow for database work. The access speed of 1990's biggest disks is 15 milliseconds!

Even if all you can afford is a vintage 10-megabyte disk, the upgrade from floppy to hard disk makes sense. But if you're upgrading an older PC, you might need to change your power supply to handle the additional electrical drain. Although a new power supply will probably cost you less than $75, this additional cost points to a second maxim: Few upgrades are self-contained. Most call for hidden extras that pump up the real costs of your makeover.

If you don't buy a hard disk card that combines a small hard disk on a plug-in card with a controller, another hidden extra involved in adding a hard disk to your computer is the cost of a new controller card to link the hard disk to the central processing unit. The controller card must match ("be compatible with") the hard disk. The $50 to $200 you'll spend for a new controller card and the $75 you'll spend for a new power supply just sent the price of your new hard disk up about $125 to $175 dollars.

Worse, you might push your machine out of the market. Once you make a change to a fundamental component, you must expect buyers to mistrust your living room engineering, especially if your computer now has a "Brand X" hard disk transplant. Read on to learn more about true costs.

Higher Density Floppy Disk Drives

These days, the list of drives available for IBM PCs and compatibles reads like a Chinese menu. For Apple computers, the choice is mercifully limited to a few standard items, but even for the Mac, you'll find numerous upgrade choices.

For the IBM PC and compatibles, you can pick from 360KB 5.25-inch floppy drives, 1.2MB 5.25-inch floppy drives, 720KB 3.5-inch floppy drives, and 1.44MB 3.5-inch floppy drives. In the new market, you can buy these drives for $100 or less—they're inexpensive upgrades. The original Apple II computer had 143KB 5.25-inch floppy drives, and you could use multiple drives with the machine. For the Macintosh computers there were 400KB drives, 800KB drives, and then Unidrives that read data on the earlier drives.

Of all the choices among IBM PC compatible drives, the most sensible one for you is the drive size your coworkers or associates use. If the office uses IBM PS/2s with 3.5-inch drives, your home computer should sprout a 3.5-inch drive, too. Similarly, when you add a laptop to your life, you need to add to either the laptop or your desktop computer a drive that allows easy disk transfers between the machines. You can buy hardware-software kits such as LapLink, Fastwire, or Brooklyn Bridge to hook your laptop to your desktop machine via a cable, but these kits require that both machines be at the same site. If the desktop resides at the office and the laptop is on the road or at home, you'll need to carry disks back and forth. The wise upgrade is to maintain compatibility with the other computers around you. Which drive size should win? Let the majority rule.

If you do decide to upgrade, be aware of the hidden costs. You'll probably need to buy a new floppy disk drive controller card to connect the floppy drive to the CPU. In the back of computer magazines, you'll see ads for general computer parts suppliers and can generally find controllers for under $50. If you have an older computer, you'll need a hardware kit for installing the drive in your drive bay. Older computers were designed for "full-height" floppy drives, which stand 3.5 inches high. No modern manufacturer makes full-height floppy drives anymore. To mount the newer "half-height" or "third-height" drive, you'll need a special mounting rack and a faceplate to plug up the remaining space. If the space is left open, air won't flow through the system properly, and the internal heat of the machine might "fry" components. The mounting hardware costs about $20.

Finally, if you go for a high density disk drive, you might need a special software "patch" so that your computer will be able to recognize the drive. The cost? Again, a nominal $10 to $20, but it all adds up. Your $100 or so investment for a new floppy disk drive has suddenly doubled!

Memory

If you still use an IBM or compatible computer with 256KB of RAM (random access memory), you can't run very many of today's programs—new software capabilities come at a price. For the first generation of IBM PCs and Apples, upgrading memory is cheap—you can buy off-brand memory boards for well under $100.

At the very least, get your memory up to 512KB—640KB would be better. You can find boards to upgrade your machine to 3MB or 4MB of expanded memory, but it's absurd to increase a first generation computer to that level of RAM. The processor won't be able to make very good use of the additional memory. If you must work with megabytes of data, step up to a 80286 or better processor.

Monitors

The jump from monochrome text display to an analog monitor that displays thousands of colors is as alluring as the leap from floppy disk to hard disk. If all you do is word processing, though, you won't need anything more than a crisp monochrome monitor. But if you use a variety of fonts and want to see them on screen before you print, or if you want to see your end-of-month spreadsheet as a graph, upgrading to a good graphics monitor makes sense. Right now, you can spend anywhere from $400 to $3,000 for a new graphics monitor, or from $250 to $2,500 for a used graphics monitor.

Caveat Upgrader! As you might suspect by now, you can't just plug a high resolution graphics monitor into your old display adapter card. You must buy a graphics adapter card that matches the capability of both the monitor and the computer. A graphics adapter card adds $100 to $5,000 to the cost of your new monitor. Each generation of graphics adapter cards offers higher resolution than the earlier one, at a higher price. On IBM and compatible computers, the original CGA (Color Graphics Adapter) card could display 640 by 200 black and white pixels, and the resolution dropped to 320 by 200 pixels for color. The EGA (Enhanced Graphics Adapter) card heightened resolution to 640 by 350 color pixels. Then came the PGA (Professional Graphics Adapter) card with a resolution of 1024 by 768 color pixels. That fizzled because of the high cost of the monitors, and the VGA (Video Graphics Array) card with a resolution of 640 by 480 color pixels became the new standard. As adapters change, who knows what will be available in the months and years to come? Pixel madness suggests that your quest won't end until resolution gets so fine that you won't be able to distinguish one dot from another.

Processors

The heart of the computer is the microprocessor. You can enjoy phenomenal improvements by switching from a first generation processor to a second or third generation processor. A first generation IBM PC runs at a clock speed of 4.77 megahertz. After you toss a 286–based accelerator board such as a Microsoft Mach 20 into your PC, your machine will soar to a 20-megahertz clock speed. If that doesn't satisfy you, you can spring for a 386–based accelerator board—Intel's Inboard 386/PC add-in board, for example. This will jack up the clock to 16 megahertz and offer as much as a 1000 percent processing speed improvement for some applications. For many users, this is a perfectly acceptable plateau in their computing evolution. Be aware, though, that you might not reap the performance benefits of an advanced chip; other factors, such as bus width, drive access speed, and the amount of fast memory, can limit the machine's performance. Depending on your task, one of a number of components can be a major bottleneck in your computer system's performance. Only a processor-intensive task makes the best use of the processor upgrade.

If the task is disk intensive (that is, the computer must constantly search for data on the disk and bring it into memory) or if the task calls for large programs or operating systems, you really need to rebuild the whole machine to achieve optimal performance. You must replace the entire motherboard (the main platform, containing the processor, memory, support chips, and the bus expansion slots), which means coughing up some serious money. With the wider bus of a new motherboard, you'll need a new hard disk controller card to take advantage of the increased data flow. You'll then need a new and faster hard disk to take advantage of the new disk controller card.

In short, you'll pay a lot of money for premium components. At that point you'll definitely have crossed into the realm in which you might as well get another machine. You've also crossed into the realm of full-blown Upgrade Mania Syndrome and might be beyond hope. By the time you replace the bus, you've effectively taken your VW chassis and outfitted it with the transmission, engine, and steering system of a Ferrari V12 Testerosa. And how safe will you feel cruising the autostrada at 160 miles per hour in your VW makeover? At a critical juncture, will you find yourself uneasy about whether you've adequately upgraded the brakes? If you want a Ferrari, save your dough and buy the real thing.

If you make all the upgrades we've talked about, you'll replace virtually everything in your computer except the serial number and the paint on the case. Any of these improvements by itself might be the most cost effective way to squeeze some additional use out of your machine. Two might make sense. There's no point in replacing the processor, for instance, without adding a hard disk. Beyond two upgrades, you must stop and ask yourself, "Does this make sense in terms of how much I'll invest for what I'll achieve?" Chances are, the answer will be "No."

EXCESSIVE UPGRADING

Two forces dictate against excessive upgrading. The first is economic, and the second is technical.

THE LAW OF DIMINISHING RETURNS

The fellow who pushed a shopping cart's worth of three and four generations of computing into the Boston Computer Exchange certainly represents an extreme. Most people don't invest $14,000 in strap-on hardware. But many people share his naïveté about the market value of his investment in upgrade equipment. Many people think that if you start off with a first generation dual drive PC (valued at around $400 in 1990) and then pop in a hard disk and a late model motherboard (about $1,400 at 1990 street prices), you'll have a late model PC.

Wrong—you'll have a souped up, first generation PC, which might add another few hundred dollars of value to that base figure.

Market value plummets the second you take add-on options and accessories out of their packing cartons. In two years, they'll lose 50 percent of their market value. This might seem unfair, given the fact that add-ons can enable your computer to do more and to do more for you, but the reality is that you'll never see a full monetary return on your investment when you go the upgrade route.

To discover the poor resale value of add-on options and accessories, let's rummage through our friend's shopping cart. In the table below, you'll find the purchase price of each item and its 1990 market value. You won't need an advanced statistical program to determine that on the average the market value of options and accessories drops 50 percent within two years. If the numbers don't make your eyes glaze over, you can readily see that your return on investment will be pretty poor.

Item	New price	1990 market value
IBM PC Motherboard	$1,200	$ 50
160/180KB Floppy Disk Drive	300	0
320/360KB Floppy Disk Drive	400	75
10-MB Hard Disk Drive	3,400	200
20-MB Hard Disk Drive	3,000	400
Floppy Disk Controller Card	300	0
Monochrome Monitor/Card	600	125
CGA Monitor/Adapter	1,000	200
EGA Monitor/Adapter	1,300	350
286 Motherboard Upgrade	1,000	500
Multifunction Board	500	100
Extension Chassis	1,200	100

Table 2-1.
Add-on options and accessories, their prices new,
and their market values in 1990.

Macintosh owners overindulge in upgrades, too. The Mac was originally conceived as a sealed box, but the add-in makers lost no time in designing all sorts of devices to add "under-the-hood" for micro hot-rodders who want the equivalent of chrome headers, quad-port carburetors, and a jacked-up rear end.

One customer of the Exchange owned an "original" 128K Macintosh and strove in vain to keep up with the evolution of the Macintosh platform. First she upgraded to the 512K memory level so that she'd have a machine "like a Fat Mac." Then she upgraded again to an 800K drive to get the equivalent of a 512e. Next, she sprang for a one-megabyte memory board to emulate a Mac Plus and followed that up with a Hyperdrive (an internal hard disk for the Macintosh). The frosting on the cake? A "scuzzy" (SCSI) port so that she could add more components and network connections later on. (A SCSI port— Small Computer System Interface—is a tool for extending the bus.)

By the time she'd added the SCSI port, this victim of Upgrade Mania Syndrome had run out of upgrade potential. The next generation of the Mac, the SE, had *internal* expansion capability. She couldn't live without that. She decided to bag the whole system and move up to an SE. As she tried to sell the mishmash she'd put together, buyers would read the description of the layers and layers of hardware and say, "Hmm… a 128 Mac with a *lot* of upgrading!" They bid for the base system and gave the upgrades practically no value.

By now you get the message: Don't invest in a total upgrade as a means of getting a "cheap" high powered computer. It won't be cheap, and you'll never get back your investment. You might have no choice if all you can afford are incremental additions to your system to get the power you need. Go into the makeover with your eyes open. Don't expect much ultimate return on your investment. And be prepared for a few potential hardware problems along the way.

HARDWARE FOLLIES

A computer is like a chain—it's limited by its weakest component. If you buy a state-of-the-art processor to replace your original processor, you will realize only a fraction of the potential power offered by the state of the art.

Let's say, for example, that you buy Intel's Inboard 386/PC add-in board to enable your first generation 8088 PC to masquerade as an 80386–based PC. Does the old 8088 machine perform as if it were an 80386 machine? Yes and no. In terms of sheer processing speed, the old PC truly has new life; the first time you turn on your beefed up 8088 machine you'll think it's a ballistic missile. But the data is still transferred via the bus in 8088 terms (8 bits at a time), not 80386 terms (32 bits at a time). Data flows to and from the disk drive, video display, and expansion bus at tortoise speeds relative to the processor's. The result? A hybrid between a first and a third generation computer.

Is that so bad? For word processing and spreadsheet computing you'll notice dramatic improvements in some areas and nominal differences in others. For database applications, which tend to be extremely disk intensive, the performance of the homegrown upgrade will be mediocre compared to that of a real third generation machine that has a processor with a matching bus, hard disk, and video graphics display.

And sometimes, the inappropriate mix of components can create bizarre problems. We know of one owner who beefed up his early model computer by adding a faster clock crystal in the hopes of setting a new land speed record in personal computing. This lead to an "autoimmune reaction" in which the hard disk rejected its own processor, making the data on the disk inaccessible to the computer. The processor expected the hard disk to respond at the new high speed, but the disk chugged along at its original pace. After a weeks-long effort to diagnose the hard disk's problem, the owner realized that the mismatch of components was the real culprit. In an effort to save microseconds, he'd wasted macro weeks.

Finally, some peripherals (and software) simply perform unreliably on "kludge" machines. Coauthor Bennett at one time could have been nominated "Kludge Master of Boston," possibly even "Kludge Master of the Western Hemisphere." His "shopping cart" contained a first generation PC he'd upgraded innumerable times into a hybrid beast that would make Dr. Frankenstein drool with envy. He had a high powered processor, but his tape drive wouldn't format tapes unless he slowed the computer down to its original 4.77-megahertz clock speed, thereby defeating the whole purpose of the upgrade. Some programs simply refused to run on the hybrid. He also discovered that, depending on the twists and turns of the cable from the upgrade processor board to the old motherboard (which contained the old processor and the bus), his machine might or might not generate peculiar interference with his monitor. He had to consult a detailed sketchbook of the "correct" twists and turns of the cable each time he opened the cover. Eventually, he got sick of doing a fandango through a mine field and sold the whole apparatus for a fraction of his investment. Then, he ponied up the money for a true third generation computer. His problems ended immediately.

The biggest problem with the "kludge factor" is that you don't know what problems you'll run into until you run into them. PCs support only a limited number of add-ins in the first place, and a vendor can't assure customers that her product will work in a system with all other vendors' products. No technical support person at any of the manufacturers is capable of tracking all the exponentially increasing possible add-in combinations and their potential for conflict. You might find yourself bounced around like a ping-pong ball as your phone calls to tech support lines elicit, "Hmm, that's interesting, haven't heard of any trouble with anyone using our board and a HyperVentilator board—it must be some conflict with that other gizmo you got from TachyCardia Systems. Better give 'em a call. You folks have a nice day."

You end up the only expert on your system, and no one wants to buy *that* particular combination of components. The evolutionary offspring of your original machine will be a true individual, as unique in its behavior as children are. It might be perfectly well-adjusted and never give you a moment of grief. It might occasionally keep you up through the night as you try to nurse it through a colicky period. Or it might be utterly obstreperous, eternally stuck in the "terrible twos."

The bottom line is clear: If you need a state-of-the-art computer, go out and buy one. If it will really enhance your productivity, you should be able to justify the cost to your boss, your banker, your husband or wife, or your mother. If you've just been asked to produce 14 company newsletters and 50 technical bulletins, you'll need the fastest, most powerful machine available and the largest, highest resolution graphics system money can buy. You can justify the cost in terms of higher quality products with faster turnaround time.

If you're a consultant and you need state-of-the-art equipment for analysis, sophisticated graphs and publications, or custom programs, you should ask yourself, "Will the machine enable me to do work I couldn't do with the computer I have right now?" If it will, ask, "How long will it take the new machine to pay for itself?" And, "Will the new computer save me significant amounts of time?" If the cost seems justifiable to you, you'll find a way to buy the machine you need. If you can't justify the additional expense, you don't *need* state-of-the-art technology; nor do you need a state-of-the-art hybrid monstrosity.

But let's be honest with ourselves—many computer purchases are based on computer machismo, not rational decision making. We are all, to some extent, swept away by the dazzling ads that promise great speed and power. (Notice how many ads use images of rockets and jet fighter planes?) If you want the thrill of more thrust, wait until a new generation hits the street (doesn't take long these days) and prices drop on the machine you've set your sights on—true love will endure the test of time. As you'll see, you might well be able to buy the system of your dreams from another rocket jock who's just found a quicker way to get from the DOS prompt to Alpha Centauri.

Randall's Rules

↔ Don't replace a single component with one that's too powerful for the other components in the system.

↔ Watch out for hidden costs when you upgrade.

↔ Maintain compatibility with other computers around you.

↔ Spend a lot less on upgrade parts *in toto* than it would cost you to replace the system. A 256KB IBM PC is still a 256KB IBM PC—even after you dress it up in sunglasses and running shoes.

↔ Add to a system rather than replace core components.

CHAPTER 3

TWO BITS FOR A BYTE

Establishing Fair Market Value
for a Computer

◆▸

Randall's Notebook

January 19, 1984

Boston, Massachusetts

◆▸

Call from Thelma C. in South Carolina. Thelma's just received a letter informing her that by visiting a vacation time-share unit in Orlando, Florida, she's "guaranteed" to win one of four prizes, the least valuable a brand-name computer worth $2,000. Coincidentally, that's the precise amount the week-long time-share deal will cost her.

Now, Thelma is "no fool," she tells us. She's read the fine print on the back of the letter and knows that the chances of winning anything but the computer are pretty bleak. So she plans to finance her vacation by selling the computer through the Exchange. Who knows how she heard about us.

The conversation between Thelma and John F., the broker who handled the call, goes something like this:

"What kind of computer do you want to sell, ma'am?"

"I don't know—it's just a computer. They didn't say exactly, you know, just that it's got 64 rams, and it's worth at least two thousand dollars."

"Well, there's no way I can tell you what its resale value is without knowing more about it. But if you want to get the maximum price, don't open the box. If you cut the tape, the price tumbles."

"So you can't tell me what it's worth?"

"No, ma'am, sorry—not without knowing the make, model number, type of disk drives, type of monitor—that kind of stuff."

"Huh? That's a cryin' shame—I was thinkin' about takin' a two thousand dollar loan from the credit union to buy a week at the vacation condominium and then sellin' the computer to pay back the loan."

"I wouldn't do that, ma'am. Computers often aren't worth what you think they are."

Too bad for Thelma. She got the loan anyway, bought her week in the time-share condominium unit, and got her "free" prize—after she paid the $100 shipping and handling fee. When her computer arrived, she sent it straight up to us for appraisal. Guess what was inside? An Osborne I worth $100 on the Exchange! Osborne had stopped production of the machine, which was why the time-share scammers were able to pick up carton-loads of the computers for a song. Yes, once upon a time they did sell for nearly $2,000. But what's a little act of omission between friends? They can always hash it out poolside.

❖

GUT FEELINGS AND HEARTTHROBS

Thelma's case is extreme, but it painfully illustrates a key concept in determining fair market price for used computers: Emotions drive value. Thelma wanted the computer to be worth a certain amount so that she could live a dream beyond her means. Even though she represents a small percentage of computer sellers—people who have "stumbled" into a computer and wouldn't know a DOS prompt from a cue ball—in some ways, she's typical of today's sellers. Even people who use computers every day get emotional about them. A seller who likes his old XT but needs more horsepower expects the XT to be worth close to what he originally paid for it. Or the opposite might be the case: Someone who feels that only a 33-megahertz Compaq 386 will serve her needs might think that her "old clunker" is worthless.

Someone who wants to buy a particular computer often gets emotionally attached to the *idea* of that machine. Even a ridiculously high price for the computer of his or her dreams might seem to be justified. And a buyer might believe that just-past-state-of-the-art models are ready for donation and should be available "on the cheap."

Because "fair" is a subjective notion, determining fair market values for used computers could be a difficult task. Fortunately, some 200 years ago, Adam Smith gave us a theory for understanding the forces behind any marketplace, including the one for secondhand computers. Adam Smith's "invisible hand" gently guides the valuation process for computers along rational lines. Here's how it works: If we had perfect information and an infinite number of trading partners for one computer model, every seller would know what every buyer was willing to pay, and every buyer would know what every seller was willing to settle for. In such a state, everyone would arrive at the same figure, which would be the machine's fair market value.

Fair market value is a matter of consensus. For a transaction to occur, at least one buyer and one seller must agree on a machine's value. Our friend Thelma would have been fine if there had been a consensus that the Osborne I was worth $2,000. Unfortunately, no buyer was willing to agree with her belief in the value of the machine.

Every market situation is unique, but by observing many thousands of transactions, we can distill a general set of principles for determining fair market value for used machines at any time. Before we discuss those principles, be aware that there are no pat formulas for valuing a machine; it is simply impossible to say that a four-year-old IBM AT with 512KB of memory is worth x times $(y - b)$ or that an Apple Mac II with a 40MB hard disk is worth $(z - x/r)$ times the change in your pocket. Any article or book that advocates such formulas or that claims to provide accurate, fixed prices will be either grossly wrong or grossly out of date. Even blue books can be out of date by press time. The market simply moves too fast, and there are too many variables for anyone to be able to develop valid formulas. Still, by applying the *general* principles described in this chapter, you can get a good idea of what to expect in the secondary market.

THE CAM CURVE

Personal computers, regardless of make or model, follow the same course as they lose market value. This pattern of market value loss, which is graphed in Figure 3-1, we call the "Cam Curve" (named after Exchange cofounder, Cameron Hall, who discovered the phenomenon late one night while analyzing the database). The Cam Curve moves through three phases: Initial Plunge, Gradual Decline, and Base Value. The slope of the curve varies for different makes and models, and the Gradual Decline is often slowed by plateaus and punctuated by sudden declines. Even so, the essential pattern remains the same. Let's take a look at what transpires as a computer's value slides down the Cam Curve.

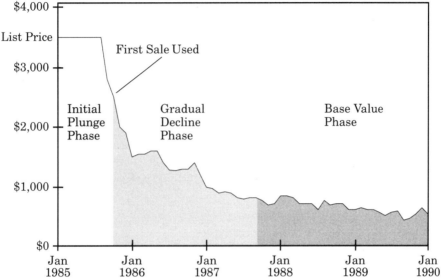

Figure 3-1.
As this generic Cam Curve, based on monthly data points, shows,
the price steadily ratchets down over the life of a computer.

PHASE 1. INITIAL PLUNGE

In the Initial Plunge phase, the market value of a new computer drops from its retail price to its price when it appears in the secondary market. The computer enters the secondary market the very moment you open the box, at which point the computer is no longer "new." Just as the value of a new car plummets the moment you drive it off the dealer's lot, a computer loses 15 to 40 percent of its value when you open the box.

Extreme circumstances can dramatically alter the value loss percentage. If a computer model is in high demand and hard to find, it might sell near its retail price in the used market. If there is little demand, or if the computer's an off-brand model, its value after the Initial Plunge might be a much lower price than its owner anticipates.

Let's look at some factors that determine the slope of the Initial Plunge in more detail.

State of the Box

As long as the manufacturer's original tape is on the box, a computer isn't used. In fact, many retailers will take back a computer if the box is unopened but will charge a restocking fee if the tape has been slit.

In 1987, Dave T. came into the Boston Computer Exchange with an $11,000 investment in Macintosh equipment—a MAC II and a LaserWriter printer. Dave's uncle had volunteered to put the computer purchase on his VISA card so that Dave could pay it off gradually while he finished school.

Unfortunately, the day after Dave bought the computer, his uncle died unexpectedly, and Dave's aunt, who'd opposed the arrangement in the first place, wanted instant payment on the outstanding VISA bill. Dave hadn't opened the LaserWriter box, so the retail store graciously took the printer back and credited his uncle's VISA account with the full amount. But Dave had cracked the tape of the MAC II box and the store couldn't restock it, so the salesperson suggested he sell the machine through the Exchange. The best we could do was to find a buyer who would pay $5,600—a 26 percent reduction from the $7,600 charged to the VISA account. As Dave found out, when you cut the carton tape, you cut the price.

Installation

Paradoxically, installing the computer—setting it up, formatting the hard disk, ensuring that all the components work together, resolving warranty era equipment failures, and installing software—actually *reverses* the Initial Plunge by as much as 5 percent. Computer equipment tends either to self-destruct when it is first powered on or to last for many years. Getting it all to work together and configuring it as a whole system is valuable to a buyer.

(Speaking of instant failures, coauthor Bennett once turned on a brand new dual drive PC, only to see smoke trickle out the vents of the monitor. His secretary suggested using it as the office toaster, but he opted for an instant service call instead.)

Filling out the warranty card, surprisingly, has little effect on a computer's resale value. Manufacturers count the warranty period from the date on the authorized reseller's invoice, not the date on the user's filled-in card, so it's the invoice, not the warranty card, that proves a machine is under warranty. Already short warranty periods have usually expired by the time a machine hits the secondary market, anyway.

Brand Name

As you might expect, brand-name computers hold value far better than off-brands, or "clones," do. IBM's AT was the flagship product of a reputable company. Consequently, when the first used AT appeared in the Exchange database, shortly after the official AT debut in computer stores, buyers were already queued up at the Exchange to pay near retail prices for used models. Look at the Cam Curve for the first year or so of the AT's life in Figure 3-2 on the next page.

Because of brand-name recognition, IBM equipment generally takes only a slight Initial Plunge and the slope of its decline toward Base Value is usually gentle. Notable exceptions to this pattern are the ill-fated PCjr and IBM Convertible, which took steep dives and fetch only nominal used prices today. If a PC isn't a hit in the primary market, it won't be a hit in the secondary market, either—even if its name plate is prestigious.

Computers can have interesting careers on the Cam Curve. The first Leading Edge Model D to pass through the Exchange traded for almost 40 percent less than the retail price. Leading Edge was just an off-shore brand then. After *Consumer Reports* magazine ran a laudatory story on Leading Edge, people lined up to get their hands on the Model D. Suddenly, the product had respectability and brand-name recognition. But the darling of the industry fell into disfavor when the company went into Chapter 11 reorganization a few years later.

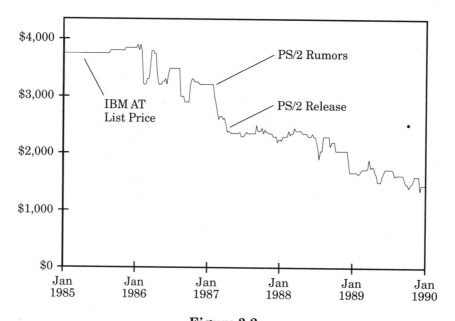

Figure 3-2.
In great demand, the IBM AT computer retained high resale value in the secondary market. Note in this graph based on weekly data points that much of the AT's value was lost between the rumored announcement and the actual release of the PS/2.

Available Supply

The Initial Plunge is also affected by the availability of the computer model. When the supply is tight, as was the case with the Toshiba T-3100 laptop at its introduction, the model commands a price in the secondary market comparable to its new retail price. The collective action of buyers scrambling to find Toshiba's fancy laptop quickly drove its used price up to near–retail price. For several tight-supply weeks, new units were sold at a premium *above* retail list price and used units commanded prices close to the new retail list price. Cases as extreme as the Toshiba laptop's are rare, but they can occur because the components of cutting edge technology—processor chips, for instance—can be hard for manufacturers to obtain.

When a model is amply available on the new market and discounters engage in mutually destructive price wars, the market value of used units in the secondary market erodes. Buyers shop the discounters, and sellers of used models must offer better prices than the best discount prices for the model. The Initial Plunge can be a shock to a seller if she paid dearly for a model that later becomes readily available and heavily discounted. This is all straight Economics 101—the PC revolution has not repealed the law of supply and demand.

Moderating the Initial Plunge

→ If you fall into a computer by accident (a gift, a prize, a deceased relative) and want to sell it immediately, *don't uncrate it!*

→ If you think you'll routinely buy up to keep in step with changing technology, buy brand-name computers. If you can't afford a brand name, wait—or find a way to finance one. Clones offer short-term financial benefits but will cost you big bucks when you try to sell them.

The experience of the Boston Computer Exchange has been that people by and large want brand new clones or used name-brand machines. People's inhibitions about used machines are raised to an even higher level when the equipment doesn't carry a well-known brand name.

If resale isn't a concern, by all means buy a serviceable clone. If you do care about a machine's resale value, remember that a clone, even one functionally equivalent or even superior to its name-brand counterpart, won't hold its value at resale time.

Critical Reaction

The market's initial response to a computer has a tremendous bearing on the extent of its Initial Plunge. Compare the Initial Plunges shown in Figure 3-3, of the IBM PC and the Apple Lisa. The introduction of the PC legitimized the personal computer market, and the PC's Initial Plunge was modest.

At the Apple Lisa's introduction, critics heralded the computer as an exciting departure in personal computer architecture but thought it was vastly overpriced. The Lisa's Initial Plunge was steep—it lost more than 50 percent of its new retail value.

DEC touted its Rainbow computer as a technological breakthrough with the highest performance/price ratio on the market, but the Rainbow was not quite compatible with the IBM PC standard.

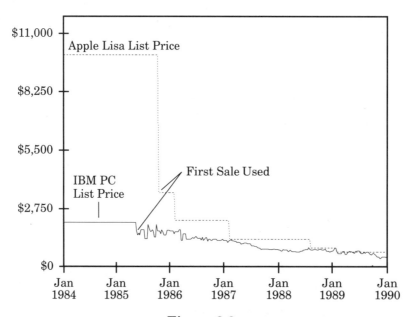

Figure 3-3.
The Initial Plunges of the IBM PC and the Apple Lisa, illustrated by weekly data points in this graph, reflect critical reactions to their introductions.

One year after IBM had established a generic technology with the PC, DEC tried to push a proprietary system. The Initial Plunge of the DEC Rainbow was a whopping 40 percent, disheartening for anyone who paid the list price of $3,495 in 1982. Wang ran into the same compatibility trap with their PC, and the machines lost more than 40 percent of their original value when they hit the secondary market.

PHASE 2. GRADUAL DECLINE

After the Initial Plunge phase, a computer's value erodes gradually to its Base Value and, ultimately, its scrap value. At the end of the Gradual Decline phase, the computer will have lost about 90 percent of its original retail value. The slope of the decline is determined by a number of factors that either slow or hasten the computer's loss in market value.

Factors That Slow the Gradual Decline in Value

Both the manufacturer and third parties can contribute to a computer's holding its value through the Gradual Decline phase.

Manufacturer's commitment. The manufacturer's plans to produce the computer or variations of the computer (as well as spare parts) over time have a major impact on how long a particular machine retains its value. For an instance of exemplary commitment, look at the Apple II family. Apple continues to manufacture variations of the original Apple II and to enhance the original "Wozniak design." And the corporation continues to offer replacement parts for the original machines.

In stark contrast are the fates of the Apple Lisa, the Apple III, and the IBM PCjr, orphaned soon after their rejection by the marketplace. Apple dropped the Lisa and the Apple III, and IBM abandoned the PCjr, leading to an instant decline in the used market values of those machines.

Third-party support. A computer's market value is also affected by third-party vendors' plans to develop and produce add-in boards and accessories and by the software community's commitment to create new programs and enhance old ones for the machine. Again, the Apple II is an outstanding example. External commitments have preserved the Apple II's value over the long term. A widespread and deeply entrenched network of third-party companies continues to create accessories and software for the Apple II, ensuring Steve Jobs's claim that "the Apple II will live forever."

Another family seemingly gifted with eternal life is the IBM PC series—the PC, the XT, and the AT. Even though IBM has stopped production of these models, a vast third-party network continues to make add-in boards that fit the PC's and the XT's 8-bit bus and the AT's 16-bit bus, and software vendors all over the world regard the PC family as an industry standard. The effect of all this third-party activity has been to slow the Gradual Decline of the PC, XT, and AT, so that the curve plateaus.

Factors That Hasten the Gradual Decline in Value

A manufacturer who enhances an old model, introduces superior technology, abandons an old model, or goes out of business hastens the gradual decline of the model's value in the used market. The speediest decline of all is brought on by the success of a new, incompatible standard technology.

Minor model enhancements. Minor changes improve performance but don't make earlier models obsolete. When IBM boosted the clock speed of the AT from 6 megahertz to 8 megahertz, for instance, the value of the 6-megahertz machine dropped, but not significantly.

Another common minor enhancement is adding larger capacity hard disks to an existing model. The IBM XT premiered with a 10-megabyte hard disk that was followed closely by a 20-megabyte version. The machines equipped with 10-megabyte disks dropped a few dollars in market value as a result, but the introduction of 20-megabyte disks had little impact on the actual performance of the XT. Such minor changes induce some buyers to sell their old models, but they don't change the buying atmosphere around the old model much.

The evolution of secondary market values for the Apple Macintosh family shows how new model introductions affect the Gradual Decline phase. In Figure 3-4 the slopes of the curves for the 128, the 512, and the Mac Plus are almost the same. None of the models completely displaced the earlier models; new models only pushed the demand for the older models down temporarily. Note that the Cam Curves for the three machines are nearly parallel.

Major model enhancements or new model. A manufacturer's introduction of a major improvement or a whole new model generally has a profound effect on the resale values of earlier models.

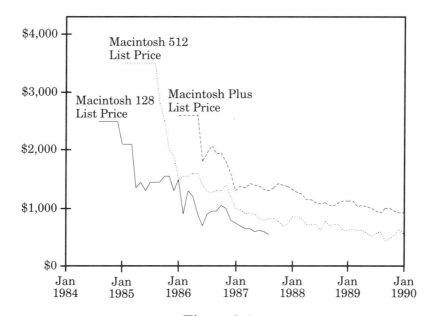

Figure 3-4.
Model enhancements in the early Macintosh family didn't seriously affect the Gradual Decline phases of earlier models. (Monthly data points.)

The early, floppy disk–based Mac Plus and SE each took a nose dive when its 20-megabyte hard disk–based counterpart appeared on the market.

Superior technology. Nothing accelerates a gradual decline more than a computer's displacement by new technology. A new machine causes a ripple through the secondary market for its whole family.

The most recent models are affected the most, and the older models experience smaller jolts. The more significant the introduction, the steeper the decline and thus the faster the computer reaches the Base Value phase. Correspondingly, the introduction of minor changes to a technology tends to keep the decline on a gradual slope.

A radical decline occurs when a manufacturer introduces a new architecture. The PC didn't lose value when IBM introduced the XT, which added a hard disk without changing the architecture. Both machines were based on an 8-bit bus and the 8088 chip. But as you can see in Figure 3-5, news of the AT, with its 16-bit bus and 286–based processor, caused the PC's value to tumble.

Similarly, when the 32-bit 80386 generation of computers arrived, the 8-bit 8088 PC and XT, having been displaced twice, dropped to fractions of their original prices. The 16-bit 80286 AT also took a significant hit in value, as did the 16-bit Compaq DeskPro 286.

Production of model abandoned. When a manufacturer drops a computer model, the Cam Curve plummets. The computer abruptly leaves the Gradual Decline phase and passes into its Base Value phase, where it retains a slight value because it is still functioning. The Hall of Orphaned Computers houses such notables as the PCjr, the Dynalogic Hyperion, the TI-99/4A, and a lot of others whose makers abandoned them.

Manufacturer out of business. The flip side of the orphaned computer coin is the vanishing company. Second-tier computer companies tend to come and go because the competition is

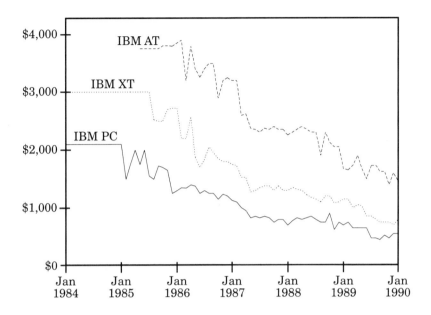

Figure 3-5.
*The 8-bit IBM XT didn't have much effect on the value of the 8-bit PC,
whereas mere news of the 16-bit AT drove the PC's value down.
(Monthly data points.)*

fierce and startups are often founded by creative geniuses who have
no business running a business. When a computer maker goes up in
smoke, the company's wares often slide straight into the Base Value
phase.

The severity of the drop depends primarily on the computer's installed base (how many are owned already). Osborne I computers, for
example, held their value for a while. The Osborne's third-party vendors and user groups kept the machine going until it lagged too far
behind current standards to run major software programs.

The whole line of Columbia Data Products fell immediately to
Base Value when the company slipped into Chapter 11. The computers still chugged away and did all they were designed to do, but
they had no significant following, and the resale value of the machines quickly evaporated. True, owners still make good use of their

Columbia computers, but few buyers will pay more than a paltry sum to take possession of a parentless child.

End of a technological era. The ultimate blow to a computer's value comes from obsolescence of the technology upon which it is based. The introduction of the IBM PC and its subsequent dominance in the marketplace effectively brought an end to the CP/M operating system. CP/M's death was slow; IBM unleashed the PC in 1981, but CP/M–based machines lived on until the mid-1980s, when

---

Scoping the Gradual Decline

➡ If you can get along between computers, the best time to sell is in the window between the announcement of displacing technology and its release. An even more far-sighted strategy is to sell at the mere *rumor* of the announcement of a displacing technology. If you want to play this game, stay on top of developments in the field.

➡ Sell your equipment at the time of its first displacement by a significantly advanced model or superior technology. You'll take a hit but not a big one. If you wait until after the second displacement, you'll experience price shock.

➡ As a matter of practicality, it is still reasonable to offer a computer for sale at the time of its second displacement by new technology. This gives you a number of years of use and a reasonable resale value.

➡ If you have a second-tier machine, one from an off-brand manufacturer, monitor the financial and computer media; if the computer maker looks shaky, sell before the company goes sour.

---

enhancement products and CP/M software faded away. CP/M computers didn't die—the market just passed them by.

Eventually, 8088–based computers will go the same route, and the timing of that event is a topic of hot debate. Someday, third-party vendors will focus on other machines and the Gradual Decline in value of 8088–based machines will reach Base Value.

But don't panic—as Figure 3-6 suggests, the demise of the first generation IBM PC computer could be years away. The PC's value took a dive when the PS/2 line was rumored, but after the PS/2s had been around for a while, the old PC's value actually rose. Limited supply and a constant demand made the PC's value increase. Third-party vendors still do a healthy business supporting the PC and the XT, and more than 16 million 8088 machines merrily churn out spreadsheets, graphs, and word processed documents. By sheer numbers alone, the 8088s might make themselves the "baby boomers" of the computer

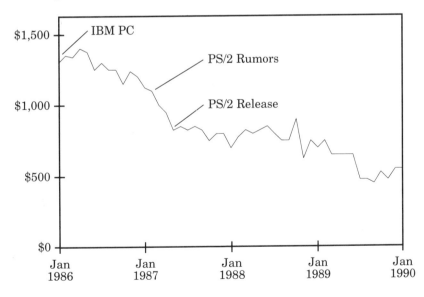

Figure 3-6.
The IBM PC's dramatic fall in market value at rumors of the PS/2 is apparent. The PC's rise in market value a year later and then again a few months after that is even more dramatic. (Monthly data points.)

world, installed in a base large enough to dictate that software developers continue to address their needs. The 8088 is likely to be around for many years to come.

PHASE 3. BASE VALUE

The last phase in the decline of a computer's value is a plateau on which the machine retains about 10 percent of its original value. We call this Base Value, a price approximately equal to what the manufacturer paid for the machine's components at the time of assembly. Analogous to a $500 VW, a computer at Base Value tends to remain at a stable price for a long time.

The factors described in Phases 1 and 2 determine how long a computer will hold some minimum value. The IBM PC and the Apple

Base Value Strategies

➥ If all you need is bare bones computing power, the Base Value phase is Bargain City. At the time of this writing, a dual drive IBM PC could be had for $400–$500, complete. If you need a computer for light letter writing, what a deal! And so much better than a typewriter! After all, a mere decade ago, thousands of cutting edge thinkers rushed out to buy that machine at original list price.

➥ If you're selling a machine in its Base Value phase, consider keeping it instead—as a backup, a specialty tool, an office bulletin board, a label maker—for some minimal task.

➥ Don't waste your time and money trying to sell something nobody wants. Donate it and take a tax write-off. (See Chapter 10.)

II will hover around their Base Values for years, sometimes increasing in value, sometimes decreasing. Other computers will make a brief pit stop on their way to oblivion. Every computer retains some value until the very last person who can squeeze some utility out of the machine has no interest in it. Most computers cease to operate before demand for them drops through the floor.

EVALUATING COMPUTER ADD-INS

By now you should have a good sense of what causes a computer to hold or lose its value. To figure out how much your machine is worth, you need to consider the value of add-ins and accessories and know a little something about the current market.

As a general rule, add-ins and accessories go through a specialized version of the Cam Curve. The Cam "Shaft" Curve aptly describes an owner's experience as the high margin peripheral he bought at retail price becomes nearly worthless overnight, despite its utility.

The Cam Shaft Curve has two phases. In the Big Plunge phase, the item loses 70 to 95 percent of its initial value. At the Leftovers Level, the product holds on to some nominal resale value. At the time of this writing, for example, a Hayes 1200-baud internal modem sells on the street (that's through discounters) for about $175. The moment you pop one into your computer, the value drops to about $90 and will stay there for as long as 1200-baud modems are in vogue. A used external 300-baud modem is worthless, and an internal 300-baud modem fetches about $25 in 1990.

Off-brand computers take a steep value dive, but off-brand add-ins and accessories really plummet when you uncrate them. A Brand X 1200-baud internal modem retailing at $99 in 1990 will have a used value of about $20–$25 the minute you take it out of the box.

A hard disk drive is like a modem in that it takes the Big Plunge right out of the box and hovers at Leftovers Level for as long as people look for one. No matter what you paid for a 10-megabyte drive in 1983, you can't sell it for more than half of what you'd pay for a current 20-megabyte drive from a mail order discounter.

Monitors become obsolete as fast as disk drives do, and their production costs are constantly falling. A monitor is like a hard disk in that it's worth the most if it's part of a whole system and worth the least if offered for sale as a single stand-alone item. A monitor without an adapter card has hardly any value at all.

GETTING GOOD INFORMATION
ABOUT THE MARKET

If you collect information from the Sunday classified ads, you won't get a good notion of fair market value—people tend to base prices on what they paid for their computers or what they want their computers to be worth. If you consult a broker, a liquidator, or a used computer store, you'll get a good sense of the value of your machine in its base configuration. The next chapter provides an in-depth discussion of information sources in the secondary computer market.

Every PC has to be evaluated in its *context*. As we've shown in this chapter, computers gain or lose value for numerous reasons and defy universal pricing formulas. You must resign yourself to aiming at a moving target. Line up your information, take aim, and shoot for the best deal you can get.

Randall's Rules

➻ Don't sweat the small innovations, but watch for major changes in the core technology.

➻ Watch the media for the overall reaction to a new model, and avoid a purchase the marketplace calls a loser.

➻ Avoid cheap clones if you want to sell later—no one's ever called the Exchange asking for a computer made up of Brand X components.

CHAPTER 4

INFORMATION CHANNELS

Finding Sellers and Buyers
in the Secondary Market

<hr/>

❧

Randall's Notebook

March 7, 1987

Chang Mai, Thailand

❧

I walk by a kiosk outside the west gate of the city and stop to read the notices on the bulletin board. Here's what I find:

- ❧ *House to rent, no pets*
- ❧ *School textbooks:* Intro to Rice Cultivation—*cheap*
- ❧ *Bicycle for sale, with basket*
- ❧ *Water buffalos, civets for sale*
- ❧ *Spiritual teachers and shamans by the hour*
- ❧ *Gem stones from Burma*
- ❧ *Herbal remedies from the Golden Triangle*

As I finish reading the last notice, an old man rides up on a bicycle and tacks a brightly colored flier over a handwritten ad for general purpose home exorcisms. The flier, complete with tear-off tabs, reads,

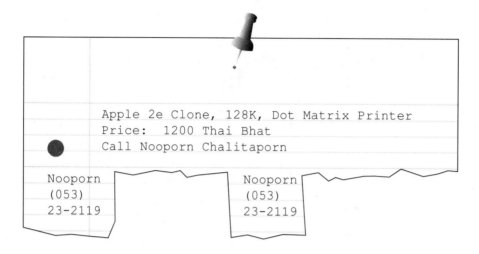

```
Apple 2e Clone, 128K, Dot Matrix Printer
Price:  1200 Thai Bhat
Call Nooporn Chalitaporn
```

Nooporn   Nooporn
(053)   (053)
23-2119   23-2119

No sooner does the ad go up than two college-age students sprint through the gate, tear off several tabs, and presumably head for the nearest phone. Quite an information channel, I think to myself. Within five minutes the seller finds potential buyers.

Twenty-four hours later, I stand in the American University Library in Bangkok, giving a speech on information management. To demonstrate the state of global communications, I log onto the BoCoEx database in Boston and search the database listings for a computer suitable for the library. Several minutes later, I print out a list of potential sellers.

On my way back to the States, it strikes me that the old man on the bicycle and I had done the same thing—only he used paper and pencil and I manipulated data bits. Both are splendid examples of appropriate technology in action!

❧

THE ELECTRONIC KIOSK OF THE 90s

All over the world, used computer sellers and buyers manage to find each other. In all cases, the same thing happens: Sellers post information about their machines and buyers see the information. In Chang Mai, the kiosk was the information channel and the flier was the information packet. In the on-line channel, anyone, in any place, at any time can post or get information about a machine.

For an information channel to work, sellers must place information where buyers will find it, and buyers must consume the information. For a transaction to take place, a buyer and a seller must become mirror images. Organized markets do the best job of bringing sellers and buyers together so that the mirroring process is most likely to take place.

The New York Stock Exchange exemplifies the organized market. Back in colonial times, a group of businessmen declared that sellers and buyers would meet on the street beside the city wall to do business. This declaration brought the information about sellers and buyers to the same place at the same time—to an organized market.

Imagine how crazy it would be to try to sell 100 shares of IBM stock by placing an ad in the newspaper. How much are the shares worth? How do you do the transaction? How do you, the seller, know that the buyer is paying the top price? How does the buyer know another seller won't sell for less? And so on. Markets grew up to answer these questions through organized trading.

In the secondary computer market, traders haven't declared a dominant market, and the result is high-level info chaos. You can find hundreds of markets, from bulletin boards in small town laundromats to on-line services in the global electronic village. They all have pros and cons, and before trading in any information channel, you should consider all the options. In this chapter, we describe the different channels and discuss their relative merits. First, though, we'll review the criteria by which we evaluate each channel.

SIZING UP AN INFORMATION CHANNEL

In order to fairly assess the merits of each information channel, we've developed a standard set of criteria.

COSTS TO USE THE CHANNEL

There's no such thing as free data. One way or another, it's going to cost you something to disburse or consume information. If you're a seller, you'll have to pay for photocopying a flier, placing an ad, or posting a listing with a broker. If you're a buyer, you'll have to buy the newspaper or want ad circular, make a phone call, or pay an on-line fee to read a listing. All information costs, even if only nominally, and how much the information costs must be factored into an evaluation of any channel.

COSTS TO DEAL IN THE CHANNEL

Finding out that a buyer wants your computer or that the machine you have in mind is for sale isn't the end of it. In some channels, you wrap up the deal yourself. If you get someone else to do the work, that person in the pipeline—a salesperson on commission, a broker, or whoever actually makes the sale happen—takes a cut.

MERITS OF THE DEAL

Not all buying and selling channels are created equal. In some, the buyer can get a great deal at the expense of the seller. In others, the buyer can pay near–list price for something that's hardly worth it. In yet others, the only winner is the channel operator.

VOLUME AND SELECTION

Each channel offers a different volume and mix of equipment. The local kiosk might advertise one computer, one brand per day, week, or month. An international brokerage will always offer a wide variety of makes and models. The more listings, the greater the chance of a fair market for both seller and buyer. The seller reaches more potential buyers attracted to the big market, and the buyer is more likely to find what he or she wants and can compare prices.

ORGANIZATION

The more chaotic the channel, the harder it is for buyers to find what they're looking for and the less likely the sale. In the most chaotic channels, the buyer trying to compare Apples with Apples and make an intelligent decision has to look through hundreds of listings. The better channels at least sort the products by type, maker, model, and price, making a good match between seller and buyer more likely.

THE SCHLEPP FACTOR

Generally, the amount of grief you are willing to tolerate is proportional to the amount of money in your pocket after the deal is done. If you're a seller willing to ferret out a buyer yourself, demo the machine, negotiate all details of the transaction, and deliver the machine, you'll make the most money. If you get someone else to do the dirty work, your payoff on the deal will be considerably less. The same applies to the buyer. If you're willing to search for sellers yourself, test the equipment, pay in cash or with a certified check (or go to the trouble of looking honest), and haul the equipment, you'll lower the purchase cost.

If your time is really valuable, doing the schlepping yourself might not be worth it to you. Let other people do the work, and pay the extra price for their efforts.

DISPERSION (THE DANDELION FACTOR)

Any child can tell you how to sow dandelion seeds—just pluck one of the infernal weeds during the seeding phase in early spring, hold it up to your mouth, and blow. This abets the dandelion's dispersion of its reproductive information.

With computers, it's not so easy. Some market channels simply don't carry your message far enough to reach that buyer who wants the very configuration you want to sell. A small scale channel (a grocery store bulletin board, for example) doesn't reach many traders. That reduces the chances of the buyer's and the seller's finding their marketplace mirror images.

Channels with a big reach can approximate perfect market conditions. A wide channel costs sellers more, but they usually get better deals because the wide channel brings in the top dollar buyers. Buyers are better off because they're more likely to find the configurations they're looking for.

RISK

Some channels are safer than others for both sellers and buyers. The seller the buyer meets through a kiosk ad might pass off a computer with a broken disk drive. The buyer might write a rubber check. A reliable computer broker or reseller has a reputation to maintain and will test and (sometimes) guarantee the computer and the check.

HIT RATE

The name of the game is "find your mirror image": the seller who has what you want, the buyer who wants what you have. A channel is only as good as its ability to find the best match among the millions of traders.

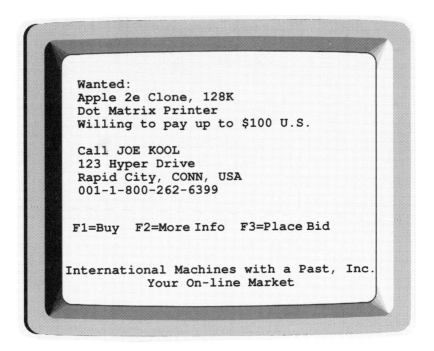

```
Wanted:
Apple 2e Clone, 128K
Dot Matrix Printer
Willing to pay up to $100 U.S.

Call JOE KOOL
123 Hyper Drive
Rapid City, CONN, USA
001-1-800-262-6399


F1=Buy   F2=More Info   F3=Place Bid


International Machines with a Past, Inc.
        Your On-line Market
```

THE KINDS OF
INFORMATION CHANNELS

The information channels we'll evaluate can be divided into four categories: print media, stores, events, and professional services. In this section, we'll evaluate each channel according to the criteria we've just described. You can decide for yourself which channel is best for you.

Note that our analyses of information channels are based on years of direct experience as well as on reports from people who have either done well in a channel or been taken to the cleaners. We tend to be skeptical about a channel that doesn't have a good track record in the secondary computer market. At the very least, heed our red flags, evaluate your local conditions, and use common sense.

NEWSPAPER CLASSIFIED AD

The seller pays for the ad, and the buyer pays for the newspaper. The ad appears for a day or a week, and the coverage is local.

Only a few computer and computer equipment ads appear in each edition, usually buried among ads for office and business equipment. The market isn't targeted: Serious buyers have trouble finding what they want, and the buyers who do call tend to be not too knowledgeable and not too serious about buying. Sellers tend to be amateurish, too, and might have little data upon which to base asking prices.

The seller must answer and filter calls, field questions, and demo the machine. The buyer must travel to the machine and test it. They must work out the details of the deal themselves with no assurances, and they must arrange for payment and hauling.

Tips

Seller

➻ Don't waste your money—business classifieds aren't cheap, and the results are often disappointing.

Buyer

➻ Call before you travel to the site. Verify that the machine advertised is the one you're looking for.

➻ Test, test, test before you buy.

➻ You'll find occasional bargains, but asking prices are usually high.

Comments

Newspaper ads are the first channel inexperienced people think of when they want to sell or buy a used computer, but they are a poorly targeted, poorly organized medium. A shrewd buyer can find an occasional bargain, but for the most part, high asking prices from un realistic sellers are way out of line with fair market prices, and amateur buyers don't know exactly what they want. The biggest problem is the medium's lack of staying power: This morning's computer ad will be this afternoon's fish wrapper. This is a good channel to avoid.

WANT AD CIRCULAR

Most cities and suburbs have one or two weekly "ad rags" distributed on newsstands or outside convenience stores and supermarkets. Generally, the seller doesn't pay for the ad until the equipment is sold. The buyer can pick up the ads for free or for a nominal cover price.

When the machine is sold, the seller pays a percentage against a fixed maximum fee for the ad (10 percent or $50, for example). The deal doesn't cost the buyer anything above the negotiated price of the machine.

The circulars reach only a local or regional audience, and serious buyers might not look for the machines they want in the unpredictable, sketchy listings of a general want ad circular. Canny computer shoppers know they'll find only a few, if any, computers after an exasperating search through a mix of unalphabetized general office equipment. Some want ad circulars don't even classify their ads.

As with a newspaper ad, the seller must filter calls and field questions from amateur, casual shoppers who don't know what they want. Then the seller must demo the machine and ultimately either put the sale at risk by insisting on cash or a certified check or accept a personal check with fingers crossed that it won't bounce.

The buyer must get to the site, test the gear, negotiate an acceptable form of payment with the seller (a trip to the bank for cash or a certified check), and haul the machine away. If the buyer doesn't spend some time testing, he or she might haul a piece of junk.

Tips

Seller

- ➳ Be prepared to answer questions.
- ➳ Be prepared to demo the machine.
- ➳ Get cash (or the equivalent).

Buyer

- ➳ Verify the make, model, and contents of the system before going to the trouble of making a site visit.
- ➳ Find out why the seller is selling.
- ➳ Never accept the first price quoted—negotiate a good price based on some comparison shopping.
- ➳ Don't pay cash for untested equipment.

Comments

Sometimes you can easily move a system or find an exceptional deal through a want ad circular. But in general, inexperienced computer sellers and buyers use these circulars, and you're better off sinking your time and energy into another channel.

BULLETIN BOARD

Bulletin boards are ubiquitous—in kiosks, campus buildings, churches, laundromats, supermarkets, and other public sites. All it costs the seller to post an ad is xerography and a thumbtack or tape. The buyer spends time and shoe leather.

With bulletin boards, anything is possible! The selection and the audience depend on where the bulletin board is. A bulletin board in a tech college is an excellent place to post and find computer ads. A bulletin board in a laundromat carries an ad for a computer by pure chance. The likelihood of that ad's finding a buyer will be remote.

Bulletin board ads aren't organized. The seller's flier gets mixed in with ads for rides to Cleveland, cleaning services, and meditation classes. Bulletin boards in campus computer departments are a little more focused, but even those ads reach only a local audience.

Seller and buyer are on their own. They must arrange to meet, demo/test, and negotiate. The buyer must test thoroughly or risk buying a lemon. The seller must insist on cash or a certified check or risk getting a rubber check. Usually the buyer hauls the machine.

Tips

Seller

↦ Focus on multiple, suitable ad locations.

↦ Be sure to provide tear-offs—as any student or nomad will tell you.

Buyer

↦ Call first. Be sure the equipment's what you think it is before you travel.

↦ Educate yourself. Comparison shop.

↦ Test it before you buy it.

Comments

A bulletin board in a technical institute or a university can be a good channel. Bulletin boards in the general community aren't a productive channel for the seller or the buyer. The seller waits a long time for the buyer ready to deal, and the buyer wastes a lot of time tracking down overpriced equipment.

COMPUTER SPECIALTY WANT AD TABLOID

These weekly or biweekly tabloids specialize in computers and computer peripherals, and they reach a national or major-metropolitan readership. The seller pays for the ad up front. Its cost varies with the size of the ad. The buyer pays the cover price.

The seller's ad will be in good company with ads for computers from major manufacturers well-organized by brand. The buyer can find what he or she wants and do a little comparison shopping at the same time. That kind of organization tends to keep prices comparable.

The schlepp factor is high for both seller and buyer. They do all the dealing themselves. The buyer has no assurances that the equipment will work, nor the seller that the check won't bounce, and they must agree on who will pay for the shipping.

Tips

Seller

- Buy the smallest ad that does the job.
- Don't accept a personal check as payment.

Buyer

- Buy as close to home as possible.

Comments

It's hard to do an interstate deal by phone without a middleperson. But a computer specialty tabloid might be ideal for selling and buying peripherals and small parts that other channels ignore.

PAWN SHOP

Pawn shops take almost anything—including computers. The seller makes an easy deal, but the payoff "loan" is usually a paltry sum. The pawn shop owner isn't likely to be up on fair market prices and usually figures that the seller is desperate.

The buyer usually pays an outrageously high price, but because pawn shop dealers aren't familiar with market prices, a lucky, smart buyer might find a real steal. That's "might." To the best of our knowledge, no pawn shop is an IBM value added reseller.

The selection in a pawn shop is sketchy at best, and the buyer must sift through tubas, guitars, radios, TVs, and fake pearl necklaces for that chance computer gem.

There are no guarantees—the buyer must find out whether the machine works and haul it away.

Tips

Seller

• Sell to a pawn shop only in desperation.

• Do consider that a pawn shop might be the only way to deal with an off-brand, nonstandard machine.

Buyer

• Try a pawn shop to find a machine to sacrifice for parts.

• Keep your eye out for a real steal, but be sure it works.

Comments

If you're looking for a cheap guitar or TV and happen to see a NeXT computer (worth $10,000), tell the pawn shop owner it's a prop from a *Star Wars* movie and offer him $50.

RETAIL COMPUTER STORE

Some retail stores take used computers as trade-ins against new equipment sales. The channel doesn't cost the seller a thing and helps defray the cost of the new computer. The buyer spends drive and browse time.

The seller does have to buy new equipment in order to trade in the old, but it can be a good deal for the seller if that's the only way he or she can afford a new system. The seller shouldn't expect a lot for his or her old equipment.

The buyer can often find a good deal as the store tries to unload the used merchandise it bought to bring in new equipment customers. The buyer might find an extensive selection, well-organized by make, on the shelves or find only a few machines.

The seller and the buyer face little risk. The seller takes away a new computer, and the buyer can count on the retail store's having tested the computer and providing at least a minimum amount of service and some kind of warranty.

Tips

Seller

- ⇥ Don't expect the store to take an off-brand computer for trade-in.

- ⇥ Trade Apples for Apples—don't take a Mac to an IBM shop. If they agree to take it at all, they'll skin the price to the core.

- ⇥ Haggle over the price of the new computer—you won't have much maneuvering room with your selling price for the old equipment.

Buyer

↝ Check the warranty—it should be for at least 30 days.

↝ Ask about service.

↝ Haggle over the used price—this isn't where the store makes their bucks. Besides, they want to get rid of the equipment—especially if they've reluctantly accepted as a trade-in a computer that isn't their main brand.

Comments

Because the store makes its money on the new computer sale, a retail store with a trade-in program is a good place to buy a used computer, but you wouldn't want to try to sell one outright there.

Trading in to buy up nicely illustrates a trade-off in terms of the schlepp factor: It's easy to do the deal, but you don't get much money. At one time IBM's dealer trade-in program, for example, offered $1,175 as the trade-in price for an AT Model 339. At the very same time, the 339 traded briskly through the seats of the Boston Computer Exchange for more than $3,000—a little more schlepping for the seller, but a lot more money, too.

USED COMPUTER STORE

Used computer stores buy the seller's machine outright and offer it for sale at a markup. The channel costs the seller telephone and transport time. The buyer spends drive and browse time.

Sellers get their money right away, but that can be as little as 50 percent of the do-it-yourself price.

Local buyers can usually find a selection of major brands and new clones displayed on shelves by make. The buyer generally gets a machine for a fair market price and takes little risk. These stores service what they sell.

Tips

Seller

- ↦ Know the fair market price beforehand so that you can negotiate with the store buyer.
- ↦ If you've got a hot model, hold out for top dollar.

Buyer

- ↦ Stores make money by moving products—negotiate hard.
- ↦ Find out whether the store's an authorized service center for the brand you're buying or whether the store has any service capability at all.
- ↦ Watch out for "bait and switch" routines. ("Hey, have I got a deal for you! Why buy a yucky old used IBM AT when you can get a brand-spanking-new St. Elmo's Turbo Flamer 286 for the same price!")

Comments

Used computer stores take a position in the market, making their money from both ends, buying low and selling high. This gives them room to negotiate, and as a seller or a buyer, you should exploit that.

CONSIGNMENT STORE

In a consignment store arrangement, the seller drops off the computer, and the store charges a commission upon sale. Placing the computer with the store doesn't cost the seller a thing. The seller drops off the computer, and the store sends a check. The buyer spends browse and drive time.

The deal itself costs the seller quite a lot—sometimes as much as 35 percent. The buyer pays nothing beyond the cost of the computer, but that can be high—whatever the market will bear—with the store's commission factored in. The store has the seller's best interests at heart in that it makes the most when the seller makes the most, but the commission does tend to wipe out the seller's benefit.

If the store's big enough, it can display a lot of computers, well-arranged by make, on its shelves. This can attract a lot of buyers within driving radius of the store who are likely to find what they're looking for. But if the seller's computer isn't in hot demand, it might sit for months in a strictly local market.

If the store is reputable, it will test and guarantee a computer. All the buyer has to do is pay for it and haul it away. The seller can rest in the assurance that the store will verify the buyer's check.

Tips

Seller

- Find out if the store has ever sold your machine's make and model, and ask for statistics on the average time it takes to sell one.

- Know your asking price and your "drop dead" price before you go in.

Buyer

- Save yourself some time—call first and ask whether the store has exactly what you want.

- Ask whether the store can service what it sells.

- Do comparisons and negotiate the price. The store's in the business of moving computers, so there's always room to bargain.

Comments

Seller and buyer satisfaction varies from store to store. Some consignment stores provide an invaluable community service and are the best option if you want to trade locally.

AUCTION

An auction can be aggravating for both the seller and the buyer. The seller, usually a company going out of business or shutting down a department, must make the arrangements and pay the auctioneer's fee. The buyer might spend a day of his or her life listening to asks and bids on lamps, desks, and teak credenzas before the auctioneer finally gets to computers.

The selling company might make only a few desperation dollars, but occasionally, if a bidding frenzy sets in and the company bought well initially, it might actually come out ahead.

An auction is usually disappointing for a prospective computer buyer. In a feeding frenzy, bidders tend to bite into each other and drive prices up to retail levels or worse, defeating the whole point of shopping at an auction.

If a large company is going out of business, the buyer might be able to choose from among a large volume of machines. Companies tend to buy one make and type, though, so the mix is likely to be bland. And really good computers from large lots are sometimes carried away by the laid-off staff just after the security guards have been fired and before the auction ever gets going.

The lots are liable to be chaotic—it's all just a bunch of blank screens to the auctioneer. Small parts, manuals, cables, connectors, and so on, are frequently missing or in other lots. We once attended a major auction in which thousands of computers were offered for bid. The monitors, keyboards, and central processing units were all offered in separate lots, making it hard to buy whole systems.

For the seller, it's a 100 percent safe deal—everything goes for a price, guaranteed cash, though possibly little cash. For the buyer, it's a 100 percent risk—the buyer seldom gets a chance to test the equipment, and there are no guarantees. All sales are final.

Tips

Seller

⇢ Keep your systems intact in one lot—don't deal with computer-illiterate auction houses.

Buyer

⇢ Monitor auction advertisements in local newspapers, and get on local auction house buyer lists.

⇢ Test before you bid; if you can't test in advance, bid at an "as is" price.

⇢ Know exactly what's in each box before you bid.

⇢ Plan your top bids in advance. Don't get caught up in a bidding frenzy you'll regret when the gavel falls.

Comments

Don't use an auction as a way to sell a single computer. They're for volume sales only. Try private sales before you get to this stage. If you're a buyer shopping for a used computer bargain, you're likely to be disappointed by the near–retail prices.

COMPUTER SWAP MEET

At swap meets and flea markets, people rent tables to display their wares. The seller pays a nominal fee for table space and sometimes a nominal commission after a sale. The buyer pays the cost of admission, if any, and drive and browse time.

The seller gets cash on the spot but doesn't usually make much more than pin money. Buyers who come to these markets expect "steals." It's strictly a local market, so prices are driven by local conditions. Sales vary with the crowds. A seller might have to haul all his or her junk home again at the end of the day.

The selection is usually all over the map—mainly off-brand clones and odd peripherals and software organized chaotically by owner or table rather than by make and model. The buyer can find an occasional great deal on old equipment, but buying's pretty risky, especially if there's no electricity available.

Tips

Seller

- ✐ Accept only cash.
- ✐ Bring all your junk—you have no idea what people might want.
- ✐ Don't spend money on a classy display.

Buyer

- ✐ *Caveat emptor!*
- ✐ Bring a wad of cash, but hold onto it.
- ✐ Wander the whole show before you buy anything.
- ✐ Don't buy until you've tested—unless you're just shopping for parts.
- ✐ Resist the temptation to buy a lot of stuff you don't really need (a second keyboard cover or an extra disk drive protector).

Comments

The upshot of a swap meet is often a shuffling of junk from one attic to another. Look at a swap meet as a place where you try to sell everything you couldn't sell through other channels or as a place to buy machines and parts you'd never find in the real world. The festive party atmosphere can be fun. You owe it to yourself to go for the show at least once.

LIQUIDATOR

Liquidators are the guys with "a truck and a check." They come to you, give you a check, and take your computer away. They buy at the lowest price and resell to individuals and stores. They sell at pretty good, wholesale used prices in volume. They're likely to sell single used units at close to retail price.

Liquidators can be a little difficult for the layman to deal with. They tend to specialize in a single manufacturer's machine or peripheral line and to deal in volume only. Sometimes they sell "close outs" by catalog or in a store.

If the liquidators test and refurbish the used machines they buy and will guarantee them, they can be a good bet. They'll often deliver, too.

Tips

Seller

↠ The first offer might be pennies on the dollar, so have price information from another channel for comparison.

↠ You're more likely to make a sale if you have lots of gear from the same manufacturer. Liquidators aren't very interested in single computers.

Buyer

↠ Be sure the liquidators guarantee that the equipment works before you buy.

Comments

Liquidators offer the least amount of schlepping for the seller. And the lowest return. Buyers can get good deals, particularly if they buy in volume, but usually get no service on the machines they buy.

LOCAL BROKER

A local broker is a telephone oriented trader who maintains a database of available equipment and matches sellers and buyers. A broker charges the seller a nominal listing fee, and sometimes the buyer must pay a small fee for a printout of the database.

The seller must pay the broker a 10 to 15 percent sales commission out of the machine's price when it's sold. The buyer often must pay an escrow charge for the broker to hold the cash until the seller has delivered working equipment.

For both seller and buyer, a brokerage is the closest approximation to a fair market in used computers. A broker will usually list lots of every make and model and maintain highly organized information indexed by make, model, configuration, and price.

The risk for sellers and buyers is low. The broker qualifies the sellers and buyers, handles the matching, and arranges the deal. The buyer might have nothing more to do than drive to the seller's site or wait for a shipment. One broker we know even has his own courier to handle deliveries. Some local brokers will test equipment, and some offer warranties and service.

Chances of a sale are defined by the marketing ability of the broker and the geographical reach of the firm. Naturally, brokers in densely populated areas do a better job for the seller.

Tips

Seller

➻ Negotiate listing fees with the broker if you have exciting equipment to sell.

➻ Ask how widely the broker disperses the database.

➻ Find out if there's a penalty for selling on your own while your machine is listed with the broker.

Buyer

→ Ask whether the broker can escrow funds.

→ Go into the market with a specific request. Asking a broker, "What do you have that's good for word processing?" is like walking into a large automobile dealership and asking, "What do you have that moves?"

→ If you're buying your first computer through a broker and you need technical help, be sure you can get support from another source — a user group, a consultant, or a friend. If you can't find a source of technical help, buy from an outlet that can give you a hand.

Comments

The local broker minimizes the amount of schlepping per dollar. When brokering works, everybody wins. Be aware, though, that prices are often constrained by local market forces. Local brokerages are good places to sell and buy workhorse computers and, to a lesser extent, the latest and greatest stars of yesteryear.

NATIONAL (AND INTERNATIONAL) BROKER

National brokers maintain large databases for many types of used computer equipment and frequently cross national boundaries.

National brokers charge the seller a nominal listing fee. Many charge the buyer a small fee for a database printout. Some offer the buyer on-line access to the database of equipment for sale.

Upon sale of the computer, the broker charges the seller a 10 to 15 percent commission and the buyer an escrow fee to hold the cash until the buyer has received the promised equipment and is sure that it works.

A brokerage on a national or international scale offers sellers and buyers a fair market. The broker matches the buyer to the seller with the lowest asking price for the machine the buyer is looking for. The selection is large within the class of computers in which the broker specializes (micros, DEC minicomputers, or dedicated gear for special systems, for example).

The brokerage organizes its listings, making it easy to search according to make, model, type, price, and often by geographical area, too.

The seller and the buyer are put to some trouble. The broker does the matchmaking and selling and clears the funds. The seller has to pack the computer and ship it. The buyer must send a certified check and test the gear when it arrives.

The risk is low for the buyer dealing with a reputable brokerage that has an escrow service.

Tips

Seller

- Get all the facts about your machine together before you call the broker—brokers are busy.
- Don't waste time trying to list low value equipment—brokers aren't interested in items that won't earn them a decent commission.

Buyer

- Know what you want ahead of time—brokers aren't in the business of helping you decide what kind of computer you want.
- Ask how to browse through the listings on your own.
- Use the escrow service. It's your assurance that you won't buy a box of rocks C.O.D.

Comments

This channel offers sellers and buyers the middle ground, a modest amount of schlepping with a good payoff. Be aware, though, that off-brand PCs and small peripherals tend to languish at brokerages. You might want to look into other channels to move these items. Note that the escrow service, which promotes good faith between long-distance sellers and buyers, might delay the seller's getting paid. It can take as long as 30 days.

PICKING THE RIGHT CHANNEL

In this chapter, you've learned about the major information channels that can connect you with the secondary computer market. Which one is best for you? Again, it's largely a matter of personal choice. Our affiliation with the Boston Computer Exchange's national brokerage gives us an unavoidable bias, but our assessments are based on years of experience and observation of thousands of transactions. We've seen dozens of different channel models in the secondary market. Some thrive and some fail. Some are best for the buyer, and some for the seller. Some are good only for the channel owner.

Whatever channel you choose, be a smart consumer. As a seller, go for the channel with the biggest reach and never lock yourself into a situation in which you're forced to give away your computer—there's always an alternative to the pawn shop. The channels vary from little work on your part with correspondingly low payoffs to hard work on your part with better payoffs. Avoid personal checks from the buyer, and don't send off your goods until the cash is safe.

As a buyer, compare prices, haggle, and never take anything untested or unguaranteed without a way to back out of the deal. A brain-dead PC and a fully functioning machine look identical until you throw the switch. We'll talk more about consumer protection in the next chapter, where we pick up the risk issue we talked about as we surveyed the channels. We'll provide specific, precautionary advice for traders in the wild and woolly secondary marketplace.

Randall's Rules

↣ Selling is about distributing information. Buying is about consuming information.

↣ Don't hunt for IBMs in an Apple orchard.

↣ Money earned or saved in a used computer deal is proportional to the amount of work you do yourself—the more you schlepp, the more you get.

CHAPTER 5

SMART BUYING

Kicking the Disk Drives
and Other Diagnostics

◆►

Randall's Notebook

December 12, 1987

Boston, Massachusetts

◆►

Nothing ruins a Monday morning more than an irate call from a buyer who claims his machine doesn't work. This one is a dilly. The guy bought a dual drive floppy disk machine with an RGB monitor. Claims the display is dead. Here's how the conversation goes:

"Of course, it's plugged in—do you think I'm an idiot?"

"No, but I needed to ask. Now, is the brightness control turned all the way down?"

"No, I turned it up and turned it down, then left it in the middle—screen's still blank."

"How about the CPU? Does the disk drive light flash when you turn the computer on?"

"Yep. The red bulb lights up, the disk whirs, the computer beeps, and then the disk drive stops spinning. But I still can't see a darn thing on the screen."

We repeat the check, nothing changes, and he demands that I see for myself. I agree to let him bring in the computer. Two hours later, he shows up, machine in tow. I ask him to set it up, watching carefully. Aha! He didn't tighten the screws on the plug connecting the monitor to the computer. I point out that the plug is loose and tighten the bolts.

Voila! *Lights! Camera! Action! And a high resolution display. Curious about why the display looks so good, I remove the cover. What a treasure trove. In addition to an EGA card, I find a 2-megabyte memory board and a 40-megabyte disk on a card. Not bad for a guy who thought he'd bought a defunct $400 dual drive floppy disk system. Some buyers have all the dumb luck!*

➤➤

TESTING 1, 2, 3

The first question people usually ask when they think about buying a used computer is, "What if it's broken?" The second is, "How can I make sure it isn't?" The answer to the first is simple. Don't buy it. The answer to the second is more complex. You have to test it. That leads to, "Who can test it for me?" The thinking behind that last question is a holdover from your experience with used cars. You pay a mechanic to check the condition of a car before you plunk down your money because unless you're an experienced tinkerer, you might end up buying someone else's headaches.

Why doesn't the same hold true for computers? Unlike cars, computers have a limited number of things that can go wrong with them. A used computer is likely either to hum along fine or not to work at all. There are no additives a seller can dump into a computer to get it to feign good health. And very few parts in a PC wear out and still work when they're close to the point of failure.

Paying someone else to check out a used computer is usually a waste. The "pros" don't rely on special equipment for diagnosing the health of a computer. Chances are, they'll just run through the simple procedures we describe below. About the only advantage in paying a third party to check out a machine is that you might be able to get a service contract against the unlikely event that the machine self-destructs the day after you buy it.

Testing computers is relatively easy. You have to be sure that each part does what it's supposed to do. The following discussion covers the most important tests and helps you evaluate the seriousness of any problems you might find. (You'll find a handy checklist to help you organize your testing activities in this chapter, too.)

POWER-ON SELF-TEST

Turn on the computer. If you're testing a floppy disk drive system, you'll see the cursor and a "wink" of the A drive as the machine self-tests. The system then looks for a "boot" file. If it can't proceed at any point along the way, you'll see an error message on the screen. If you can't boot up, the problem could be, in decreasing order of likeliness:

- A floppy disk that doesn't contain all the essential operating system files

- A defective floppy disk

- A defective floppy disk controller card

- A defective floppy disk drive

- A defective motherboard

If the disk in the A drive doesn't contain the operating system files, all you need to do is insert one that does in the drive. The defective floppy disk problem is easy to correct—have someone copy the operating system files onto a good disk for you.

If you're testing a hard disk system and it won't boot up, the cause could be, in decreasing order of likeliness:

- Improper formatting of the hard disk

- No formatting of the hard disk

- A hard disk that's missing essential operating system files

- A defective hard disk controller card

- A defective hard disk

- A defective motherboard

How do you diagnose the exact problem? You don't. Because you don't want to buy that machine. Never buy a machine that won't boot up unless you want it for scrap and plan to cannibalize it (which is still risky because you might buy dead replacement parts).

If the system boots up, you'll see a prompt on a PC screen or a smiling face on a Macintosh screen. Watch the monitor, and note any error messages that appear. IBM and compatible machines use numeric error codes. (301, for example, designates a keyboard error, 1701 designates a hard disk problem, and 201 has to do with memory codes—consult your manual or contact the manufacturer for a description of every numeric error code.) A PC usually runs through a memory check and then displays the amount of RAM plugged into the motherboard that the machine recognizes when you turn it on. Be sure the memory figure jibes with the amount of memory you believe you're buying. (A PC usually won't be able to detect and report memory on an expansion board.)

SYSTEM DIAGNOSTICS

A CPU is a "go" or "no go" component. Now that you've determined that the machine is working, run the diagnostics routine supplied with the computer. (If you're testing an Apple machine, test by running an ordinary software package you're accustomed to using.) If the seller doesn't have the computer's diagnostics disk, you can either buy one from the manufacturer of the system or use a third-party dedicated package. Diagnostics programs check out the components of the system and report any errors. A diagnostics program might find an error that doesn't grossly manifest itself in the operation of the computer and its components, so it's worthwhile to go through the exercise.

The operating system diagnostics disk reports errors as numeric codes, so you will probably have to call a service technician or buy a separate reference manual for the machine to find out what the numbers mean. If you're lucky, you might be able to call up the computer manufacturer for the information.

Any diagnostic error should cue you to put the deal on hold until you find out what the error means. If the error indicates a minor repair, negotiate with the seller to reduce the cost or to manage the repair.

FLOPPY DISK DRIVES

All floppy disk drives make some noise, ranging from a purr to a roar. The sound that warrants closer scrutiny is reminiscent of a food processor trying to grind ice cubes. That grinding noise might indicate mechanical problems, although some drives are excessively noisy by nature. The next set of tests will tell you whether the drive is vociferous by design or sick.

1. Format a floppy disk. Was the format successful? If the drive cannot format the disk, try another disk. Multiple format failures can indicate a defective drive.

2. Insert a data disk containing files into the drive you suspect is defective and use the copy command to copy the files to the hard disk or a formatted floppy disk. Then try to copy files from the hard disk or the good floppy disk drive to a formatted data disk in the suspect drive. Any errors? If you still receive error reports, try it all again with a different set of disks. Repeated failures indicate a problem with the floppy disk drive.

3. If your copies were successful, run a disk comparison. (The utility file for comparing two disks is supplied with your operating system.) Do the disks check out? They should.

If the floppy disk drive passes this set of tests, it's just noisy.

HARD DISKS

Hard disks make whirring and grinding sounds, too. Your ear alone can't tell you whether a drive is healthy or sick. The hard disk's passing the following tests is more important than the sounds it makes.

1. Try to make a directory on an IBM or compatible machine or open a new folder on a Macintosh machine.

2. Ask to see a directory on an IBM or compatible machine or a folder on a Macintosh machine.

3. Try to run a program from the directory or folder.

4. Try to copy a file from the hard disk to a floppy disk.

5. Try to copy a file from a floppy disk to the hard disk.

In addition to these simple tests, you can run any of a number of commercial disk diagnostics programs such as the Norton Utilities and the Mace Utilities, which will show you the number of bad sectors on a hard disk. Consult the diagnostics program's manual to see how their tests indicate that a hard disk's bad sector count is unacceptable.

THE "BOX"

A used machine won't be perfect. You have to expect some wear and tear. But dents can indicate rough handling or a nasty fall that might have damaged internal components. Never be afraid to ask the seller the cause of damage to the case or the finish.

If you can open the case, be sure that no boards or chips are only partially in place. And check the "fuzz factor"—a quarter-inch layer of dust can eventually build up a static charge and short out vital components.

While you're looking, make note of any boards you don't recognize. Ask the seller what each does. If problems arise later, you'll need to know exactly how the machine is configured. Your problem might turn out to be one of the mystery boards.

THE MONITOR

Now it's time to check out the monitor.

The screen. Is the glass or plastic (if it's an LCD or plasma display) free from scratches, cracks, and stains? The screen doesn't need to be perfect, but a permanent scratch in the wrong place can be annoying, especially if you work with text. Look for phosphor "burns" by turning the brightness and contrast controls up all the way. If you see a ghost of a spreadsheet or something else likely to have been left on the screen for hours, such as a main menu, the screen has phosphor burn. When bombarded with electrons from the high voltage "gun" in the tube, the burn areas won't glow as brightly as the rest of the screen, leaving dark areas on the screen.

The image. Are the characters properly shaped? If they're "squashed" or out of proportion, the monitor might need to be adjusted. If the image wavers, the problem might be interference from an upgrade component such as a tape drive or an accelerator card, or the problem might be a malfunctioning display adapter card or motherboard-mounted display chip.

The controls. If either the brightness or the contrast control doesn't work, you won't be able to adjust the screen to your viewing conditions and preferences. Play with the controls to be sure that adjustments make a noticeable difference.

The case. Check for serious cracks, although even a major chip in the monitor's finish can be a trivial issue. What counts is whether the monitor works.

THE KEYBOARD

A keyboard is generally a pretty sturdy part of a computer system. If you're running a diagnostics program, you'll want to test each key to be sure it does what it's supposed to do. If you haven't run a diagnostics program, press each key to be sure that the character that shows up on the screen corresponds to the character printed on the key. Running a word processor that takes full advantage of the keyboard will be especially useful for this test because you'll also be able to check out the Alt, Ctrl, Shift, Tab, and various special keys.

By typing with a word processor, you'll also be able to check for "sticky" keys. Speaking of which, we once saw a Compaq "luggable" that worked perfectly except for one fluke—unless you gently tapped the keyboard in the right place, the plus (+) key stuck, creating screens full of plus signs *ad nauseam*. We questioned the owner, and ıt turned out that the poor machıne had been checked with the regular baggage during a transcontinental flight. Most people have the sense to send their computers tourist class!

In addition to checking the keyboard with a word processor, look for other mechanical problems:

The keyboard cord. Turn on the computer and *gently* pull on the keyboard cord at the base where it connects to the keyboard. Does the keyboard become inoperable? Try it again, this time tugging where the cord attaches to the connector that plugs into the back panel of the computer. If the cord is damaged at either end, it will have to be replaced. On keyboards such as IBM's enhanced 101 key model, you can remove the cord from the keyboard unit. On older IBM keyboards and many other keyboards, the cord is not a stock item. You might need to buy a new keyboard. Finding someone who can make a (working) custom cord can be time-consuming, and a new keyboard will set you back $40 to $200, depending on what you're willing to settle for.

The keys. Turn the keyboard upside down and shake it. Do any keys fall off? They shouldn't. If the keyboard has LED lights for Caps Lock, Scroll Lock, and Num Lock, be sure they work.

THE FAN

If the system has passed all the tests we've discussed, you still need to check out the fan. Fans are like disk drives in that they all make some noise. You should be concerned only with excessive noise, which indicates that something is mechanically amiss. When you start or shut off the computer, does the fan sound as if you're in a heliport? If it does, it might be ailing.

The fan is crucial for maintaining optimal temperatures in a PC. Heat is the enemy of electronic components, and nothing shortens the life spans of components the way temperatures in excess of the components' operating ranges will. Check to see that all the system expansion slots are either occupied by a board or have a cover in place.

Open slots cause cooling air to bypass the expansion boards, which causes overheating and shorter component life.

Replacing the fan of a PC or compatible usually requires replacing the entire power supply. You can pick up a power supply for under $100 from a computer parts dealer and, if you know what you're doing, install it in fewer than 10 minutes. But low cost and ease of replacement are not the issues. You need to be concerned about whether the damage has already been done—whether the computer you buy will need repair in the not-too-distant future.

PERIPHERALS

Peripherals, with the exception of printers, are like computers in that they generally simply work or don't work. The only way to test them is to put them through their paces using software familiar to you. Don't get hung up on an unfamiliar program as you test. Devote your full attention to the gear you're testing.

Printer

Printers have many more moving parts than computers do and are therefore more subject to mechanical breakdowns. Even so, the most common problems with printers have nothing to do with the inner workings of the equipment. They're most likely to be, in order of descending frequency:

- A poor or incorrect connection to the PC
- Incorrectly configured software—installation of the wrong printer driver or the use of a port other than the one to which the printer is attached, for example
- The wrong cable—an RS-232 reverse cable instead of a straight-through cable, for example
- A cable with a faulty connector

Before you assume that a printer is broken, be sure that you have correctly connected and configured the software for the printer.

Laser printer. Far and away the most common problem with laser printers is improper configuration. First generation Hewlett-Packard LaserJets and compatibles can be connected to serial ports only and require that specific mode commands be inserted at the DOS level. Many people either forget to insert the commands or insert the wrong ones and then erroneously assume that something is wrong with the printer.

Unlike the older laser printers, the HP LaserJet Series II can be configured for either serial or parallel operation. Even though most people prefer the parallel interface, the printer defaults to serial. To get the printer to work, you must make a minor setting change on the printer's built-in menu panel. Many people forget to change the printer's menu, and the printer appears to be dead. This often results in a panic call to Hewlett-Packard's technical support line. Remember this as you assess a potential LaserJet acquisition.

Laser printers are generally equipped with self-tests for print quality. A laser printer in working order will show uniform character density across the page, with no breaks or smudges. If a self-printed page is uneven, *carefully* clean the corona wire. (See the manual supplied with the printer.) A dirty corona wire can't apply an even charge to the paper as it rolls through the printer, and it is the charge on the paper that attracts the toner particles. If the problem isn't resolved by a quick cleaning of the corona wire, postpone the sale and demand that the seller supply another toner cartridge before you close the deal.

If the problem persists even with a new toner cartridge, get a professional opinion before you plunk down your money. The solution might be a simple adjustment, or the printer might need an expensive replacement part. Either way, laser printers are complex beasts that can be serviced only by qualified service reps at premium rates.

As the laser printer operates, listen for loud squeaking or grinding noises. If you hear such a sound, pop open the cover and manually turn the large gear connected to the fusor roller. (Be careful—the fusor unit operates at 400°F. This high heat melts the toner particles onto the paper, creating a permanent image.) If the fusor roller isn't responsible for the noise, change the toner cartridge. If the noise goes away, you're home free.

If the fusor roller gear is responsible for the noise, the unit might be on its way out. The fusor assembly is expensive to replace (definitely not a do-it-yourself job), so consider having a qualified service rep inspect the printer before you close the deal.

The registration roller assembly, which guides the paper, can also be a source of loud squeaking and grinding noises. If it is, have it checked out by a service professional, too.

Dot matrix printer. Dot matrix and ink jet printers generally have built-in self-tests, too. Check the user manual for instructions. Look for even and properly aligned rows of printed characters. Be sure that the characters are well-formed, with no breaks. The most common problem is a recalcitrant pin on the print head. Print heads are best installed by qualified repair people—if they can find the parts for the printer.

If the printer has tractor feeds, run a dozen sheets through the system to be sure the tractors work properly. Broken locks or feed pins will make the paper slip out of alignment. But before you proclaim a tractor assembly D.O.A., be sure the problem isn't a piece of paper stuck in the platen assembly or the tractor paper guides.

Regardless of the type of printer you're thinking of buying, the acid test is whether it does what it's supposed to do. Load your word processor or desktop publishing program and print a document or two. Be sure the printed text is complete and correctly formatted.

Daisy wheel printer. The rules for checking out a dot matrix printer apply to daisy wheel and thimble printers. The good news is that malformed characters can usually be resolved with a $20 fix—a new printing element.

Modem

The only way to find out if a modem is working is to connect it to a computer and transfer a file or send and receive e-mail. As with other peripherals, the most common point of failure is not the modem itself but the connection to the computer. Port conflict—a modem tries to share address space with another asynchronous communication device—is usually the source of the problem. Try resetting the hardware switches. Another common source of problems is a phone line plugged into the wrong RJ-11 connector on the back of the modem. (One jack is for the line and the other is for a telephone handset.)

Finally, modems are often incorrectly diagnosed as sick when the software has not been configured for the correct port or the configuration switches on an external modem have not been set correctly.

Mouse

Try it out. If you have trouble with a mouse and it's the mechanical type, you might need to clean the ball. Dirt and lint can cause a mechanical mouse to perform erratically or stick. Clean the roller and then test the mouse again.

A mouse is like other peripherals in that it might not work because of bad connections or incorrectly configured software. For IBMs and compatibles, a mouse requires that the drivers for the particular mouse brand be loaded before the mouse is used with any software. Each software program must be "informed" that the mouse exists. Any slipup along the way can make a working mouse look dead.

Tape Drive

Back up and restore several files—that's the only way to find out whether the tape drive, the interface card, and the cable are working.

If you can't back up or restore files, try another tape. If you still can't get the tape drive to work reliably, have a technician check it before you conclude the deal.

Cables

Cabling is the most common source of problems with any peripheral device. Cables are easy to replace, but if they're part of the deal, you want them to be in good condition. Look for exposed wires at both ends. If the shielding is missing, your data could get garbled. Most importantly, be sure that the cables are the correct ones for the system.

Quick Test Checklist

- Boot the system:
  - ☐ From a floppy disk
  - ☐ From the hard disk
- Listen for unusual noises.
- Copy files to and from each drive.
- Run diagnostics (if available).
- Check the integrity of components:
  - ☐ Case
  - ☐ Monitor
    Screen
    Image
    Controls
  - ☐ Keyboard
    Keys
    Cord
  - ☐ The Fan

THE SYSTEM, THE WHOLE SYSTEM, AND NOTHING BUT THE SYSTEM

So far, we've discussed the testing of individual components. You must also be sure that the system works as a whole. It's easy for hardware and software to conflict and difficult to anticipate where the conflicts will occur. If the seller has configured and used all the components together, chances are it will all work in concert for you. If the seller has cannibalized parts and peripherals from various systems, be sure it all works together before you take it back home or to your office.

↦ Test all peripherals:

□ Printer
Print quality
Paper feed
Connections

□ Modem
Dial tone
Connection with other modem
File send and receive

□ Mouse

□ Tape drive

↦ Test the integrated system:

□ Connections with peripherals

□ Configuration of software with computer and peripherals

AFTER THE SALE

After you buy a used computer, remember that you'll eventually outgrow the machine you've just acquired. You'll find yourself on the other side of the fence. In anticipation of becoming a seller, follow a few simple rules to ensure that you get the maximum dollar back on your machine:

- Keep the boxes, packing materials, and manuals.

- Use a surge protector at all times. Better yet, use a surge suppressor that shuts off power if the voltage fluctuates. High voltage (a surge) can zap electronic components, and low voltage (voltage drop) can cause a hard disk to crash, which can cost you in the data bank and in the piggy bank. Best yet, spring for an uninterruptible power supply (UPS) to maintain a constant current regardless of what's happening in your power lines. If you've just bought an IBM XT for $700, it makes little sense to preserve its health with a $500 UPS. But if you've just shelled out $8,000 for a Compaq 386 with a 300MB hard disk, the $500 investment is a wise one.

- Use a screen "blanker" to prevent burning of the phosphorous coating of your monitor. Blanker programs are often included with utility software, and many are available in the public domain through bulletin boards.

- Don't etch your name in the case or remove serial numbers. Corporations and institutions often engrave their names or permanently affix asset number tags to the chassis of their machines. This is a dubious theft deterrent and guarantees a reduced price.

- Don't apply unremovable stickers to your PC. Some enhancement board makers give you product ID stickers you can put on your console or at the top of your keyboard. These stickers might make you feel better about your computer ("Hey, this isn't really just a dual drive floppy—it has a hard disk card and a 386 processor on board!"), but you won't boost the value of your computer by making it look like a suitcase that's traveled the world 13 times.

■ Don't attach gizmos to the monitor or console with double-stick adhesive. One buyer received a monitor that had served as the platform for every self-adhesive gadget on the market, including a paper holder, a notepad, a pen, and even a "Byte Basher" (a foam hammer you can use when you get frustrated with your computer). To remove the adhesive squares, the seller used a quart of acetone, which left the monitor case looking like a Jackson Pollack painting. The buyer wasn't taken with the acetone abstract expressionism and demanded a $150 reduction in price— which is what another used monitor would have cost him. The seller lost $150.

■ Finally, try living without keyboard decals or templates that have adhesive backings. If they don't come off clean, you'll see fewer dollars when you sell the machine.

Randall's Rules

➼ No boot, no bucks.

➼ Test only one component at a time.

➼ Test the integrated system in a variety of ways.

CHAPTER 6

LET'S MAKE A DEAL

Getting to "Yes"

❧

Randall's Notebook
March 12, 1988
Boston, Massachusetts

❧

Maybe it's the phase of the moon, maybe it's sunspots, maybe it's the alignment of Uranus and Neptune. Whatever it is, no one seems to be able to agree on a fair price. The buyers want real equipment real cheap. The sellers must think they're retailing new equipment. Here's the nonsense of the week.

About ten o'clock someone calls with a Macintosh—128K RAM and a 400K floppy disk drive. Not only is it more than three generations of Macs old, but you also can't even find new and public domain software in its 400K disk format. This antique will work with Mac-Write and MacPaint—great for someone just graduating from a typewriter—but it would be of little value to a serious user. What's the seller asking? A mere 20 percent less than what he paid six years ago. What's he think he's got—a BMW?

At high noon a man calls in for his boss. It's a typical situation in which the honcho tells his henchman to unload everything in the department storage closet. Buried underneath a pile of paper towel cartons he finds an extinct beast from the CP/M era. In computer technology, this is roughly equivalent to the Pleistocene age. On the corporation's books, this machine is still worth 10 percent of the $12,995 they paid for the system in 1980. But I couldn't find anyone who would pay $1.29 for the machine, let alone $1,299.

The topper of the day comes in at three o'clock. A scout master has saved up $150 from his troop's car washes, yard cleanups, and light bulb sales. He's ready to lay his cash on the table for an IBM compatible. With a hard disk and, preferably, a modem. Oh yes, and with "hi-res" color graphics, too.

Ah, I'd like to help them all, but they're not even playing in the real world.

◆▸

SETTING THE TALKING PRICE

It's a fact of human nature: When people negotiate for anything—computers, art, baseball cards—the person who mentions a price first sets the terms of the rest of the discussion. Let's look at the negotiations for a piece of art. Assume that the buyer thinks a painting is by a great master and worth $2 million and that the owner knows it's a copy of the great master's work, worth no more than $5. If the buyer with the $2 million expectation speaks first, negotiations will hover at $2 million. If the seller speaks first, he might set a price of $500, hoping the buyer's a sucker. Establishing the market value of the painting gets underway with the figure the first speaker mentions.

The same thing happens when people haggle over the price of a used computer. In the absence of fair market valuation, whoever mentions a price first sets the level of the negotiation. Negotiation breaks down if the numbers are too wildly far apart, or the seller and the buyer come to a deal. The fellow with the outdated Macintosh expressed his belief that 20 percent below the original purchase price was fair market value, so the discussion began at that level. As the seller learned about the realities of the marketplace, the deal eventually drifted down to 90 percent below the amount he had paid for the machine new.

Similarly, the expectations of the company trying to sell the CP/M machine set the starting point for that negotiation. When confronted with the reality of the market, they realized that donating the machine would actually yield a result far closer to what they had in mind than trying to sell the machine for cash would.

The scout master's $150 could hardly cover all the items on his wish list. We talked about the system he wanted, and I explained the cost. Once the realities of the marketplace sank in, he was happy to walk away with a PCjr. His other option would have been to buy from a retail shop, where his money might have gotten him a new scientific calculator.

In all three cases, reality tempered expectations, and deals were consummated.

THE WIN-WIN APPROACH

Negotiation is about satisfying both parties, about settling on a price that looks fair to both. Sellers and buyers often have different ideas about what a machine is worth, so getting advice from a neutral third party can be crucial to getting the negotiation off on the right foot. That's why blue books and brokers help to expedite deals—they temper wild expectations. A seller or buyer should bring to a negotiation a fair market appraisal by a third party who has solid data and no vested interest in the transaction. Getting the facts about the fair market price into the negotiation reduces the potential for arguments about price.

Given the ease with which a fair market price can be established, why don't all deals happen with a minimum of grief? The answer lies in people's assumptions about the nature of making deals. If you go into the deal with a "zero-sum game" attitude (for me to win, you must lose), you're setting yourself and your negotiating partner up for an unpleasant time. A seller who expects to "fleece" the buyer probably isn't going to close a sale. A buyer who sets out to "steal" a computer from the seller probably won't walk away with anything.

The real art of getting to "yes" entails a mind-set in which you believe a good deal means a fair deal. People who go into a negotiation with that attitude quickly reach a mutually agreeable price somewhere near what other people would call fair market.

The advice in the remainder of this chapter is based on the idea that traders in the secondary market can strike up win-win deals. To this end, we describe the key strategic issues for sellers and buyers.

We recommend that you read the advice pertaining to both parties, regardless of whether you want to sell a computer or buy one. The more you understand the total process, which is defined by both the seller's and the buyer's perspectives, the better you'll be at engineering a deal that satisfies everyone involved.

STRATEGIES FOR SELLERS

If you've never sold a computer before, use the strategies described here in a dry run negotiation with a buyer. The more comfortable you are with your selling strategy, the greater the likelihood of a successful sale. If you've already sold a computer or two, use the information to assess your negotiating style and to develop guidelines for improving the quality of your next deal.

SETTING YOUR SIGHTS REALISTICALLY

To set a price closest to fair market value, bear in mind that except in situations in which you are selling a cutting edge computer in short supply, you will never recover your initial investment. There are no computer equivalents to the luxury cars that hold 90 percent of their value for long stretches of time, or even increase in value as they become classics. No, the Computer Museum isn't holding a spot for your Osborne I. They already have one of each of the original models, and no high-bidding buyer at a museum covets your dusty antique.

GETTING A SENSE OF VALUE

Before going into a negotiation, be sure you have a good idea of what your system is worth. Most brokerages and used computer businesses will gladly give you a ballpark range for your make, model, and configuration. Or you can get an appraisal from a local market maker—most will sell you an estimate of the computer's value for a nominal fee.

Several publications ("blue books") list used computer values for the major brand names. Be aware that they are usually published annually and lose their timeliness as the year goes on.

A number of organizations publish weekly price reports. The *BoCoEx Index* from the Boston Computer Exchange is the oldest of the weekly price indexes. The BCE has collected price data since 1983, and since 1986, the *BoCoEx Index* has reported every Friday on the prices of equipment traded on the Exchange that week. Computer magazines, news wire services, and on-line services carry the price report, and BoCoEx affiliates publish local versions of the *BoCoEx Index*. By looking at their reports of weekly trading, they can offer you an accurate appraisal of the system you want to sell or buy.

The following table compares *BoCoEx Index* prices for the four years from 1986 through 1989. It will give you a sense of how values change for various models. Don't try to use it to assess the value of a machine you want to sell or buy today; the data is historic.

The BoCoEx Index
Closing prices on the Boston Computer Exchange
BoCoEx Index *from one, two, three, and four years ago*

Machine	Disk	1989	1988	1987	1986
IBM PC 176		$ 500	775	775	1250
IBM XT 086	10M	775	1200	1350	1950
IBM XT 089	20M	1025	1250	1600	*
IBM AT 099	20M	1625	2300	2500	3490
IBM AT 239	30M	1800	2600	2800	*
IBM AT 339	30M	1850	3200	*	*
IBM PS/2 Model 30		1450	1525	*	*
IBM PS/2 Model 50	20M	1675	2350	*	*
IBM PS/2 Model 60	40M	2800	*	*	*
IBM PS/2 Model 80	40M	3850	4200	*	*

* Insufficient volume or not yet introduced to secondary market

(continued)

continued

Machine	Disk	1989	1988	1987	1986
Compaq Portable		475	825	850	1250
Compaq Plus	20M	900	1100	1350	2100
Compaq Portable II	20M	1700	1850	1800	*
Compaq Portable 286	20M	1600	2200	2325	3200
Compaq Portable III	40M	2575	3000	4000	*
Compaq Deskpro	20M	1000	1200	1300	1775
Compaq Deskpro 286	40M	1950	2500	2825	*
Compaq Deskpro 386	60M	2750	5100	4525 (40M)	*
Macintosh 512		450	700	825	1300
Macintosh 512e		650	800	1050	*
Macintosh Plus		1025	1050	1425	1950
Macintosh Plus	20M	1350	1350	1950	3000
Macintosh SE		1800	1950	2000	*
Macintosh SE	20M	2025	2450	*	*
Macintosh SE/30	40M	2900	*	*	*
Macintosh II	40M	3450	4750	4200 (Floppy)	*
Apple IIe		475	700	700	995
Apple IIc		475	575	625	950
Apple IIgs	10M	1400	1400	800 (Floppy)	*
Apple LaserWriter Plus		2575	3100	3300	3800
Toshiba T-3100	10M	1800	1750	2600	*
Toshiba T-3200	20M	2650	*	*	*
Toshiba T-5100	40M	3425	4100	*	*
NEC MultiSpeed EL		725	900	*	*
NEC 286 MultiSpeed		1925	*	*	*
Zenith 181		900	1050	*	*
Zenith 183	10M	1375	*	*	*

* Insufficient volume or not yet introduced to secondary market

If you're selling a complete system with a specialty item such as a mainframe emulation board, an unusually large hard disk, or a very high resolution monitor, an appraiser might have to do some comparative pricing research and charge a bigger fee. If you have no idea what your computer system is worth, a professional appraisal might be well worth the cost because it will help your negotiation with a buyer to be short and simple: "I had this system appraised, and it has a cash value of...." This kind of statement usually short-circuits a lot of haggling about price.

If your computer is still available in the new or discount market, price a comparable system made up of new components. Remember that most buyers will compare your used machine to a discounted clone and expect to spend no more than what they'd pay for the same power in a new clone. The new discount market usually sets the range of negotiation.

ENHANCING YOUR MACHINE'S VALUE

If your machine has a market value lower than you anticipated, try to enhance its value. A minor enhancement might put your unsellable or low value system in reasonable demand. The average buyer keeps a few magic words in mind—"640K," "Hayes-compatible," "VGA," and so on. If your system doesn't have the specifications or components buyers expect, you might be in for a hard sell. The following small changes can influence the desirability of your computer.

- Bring the machine up to its normal configuration. If you bought a genuine IBM processor and keyboard but saved a few bucks with an *el cheapo* monitor, springing for a used, but *bona fide*, Big Blue tube could mean the difference between a sale and no sale.

- Complete an incomplete system. Sometimes a modest investment in a minor upgrade can add enough value to bring your machine up to par, but don't upgrade beyond the standard system from the machine's era.

An IBM PC with 256KB of memory won't run many recent software packages and doesn't have much value. By spending another $50 to $100 on a memory upgrade to at least 512KB, preferably 640KB, you add to the computer's value. Similarly, adding the second external floppy disk drive to an early model Macintosh might put the slow-selling computer in higher demand.

Obviously, these upgrades have points of diminishing return. The cost of adding 2 megabytes of RAM to the IBM PC would never be balanced by the additional proceeds from its sale. And it wouldn't pay to upgrade the original 128K Macintosh to the capacity of the Macintosh Plus with 1 megabyte of RAM. The system would have as much memory as a real Mac Plus, but buyers wouldn't regard the upgraded system as the manufacturer's version of the model. The cost of the upgrade might be recoverable, but you wouldn't realize any more cash than it would cost you for the upgrade component. In other words, it would be a wash.

Modest upgrades add more value than they cost. Excessive upgrades simply add their costs to the price you can ask for a system. As a rule, upgrading beyond the standard configured version of a model doesn't add significantly to its overall value.

■ Replace missing items. If you've lost a machine's manuals, order another set or find a suitable third-party guide book. Be sure all the machine's screws, nuts, and bolts are in place and tightened down. If you frequently opened the cover for cleaning, dip switch changing, or upgrading, you probably got lazy and left the screws off. This sends a bad signal to the potential buyer, so button it up.

■ Fix all broken components. People don't want computers "as is" (unless they're bidding at an auction and willing to take a risk). If the disk drive sounds like a garbage disposal, replace it; if the keyboard's Delete key sticks most of the time, get a new keyboard; and if the contrast knob is broken, order a new one—no one wants to use a pair of pliers to adjust the screen.

■ Get it all together in one place so that you can demo the system as it will be sold. You're better off showing the computer to prospective buyers as a full system, not as individual parts. It's much harder to move individual components.

If you've done everything possible to get the highest *reasonable* price for your machine, you're ready to turn your attention to its potential new owner. If your computer is at all in demand and you're not desperate, you're in the catbird seat. Run potential buyers through your "filter" and separate real buyers from the window shoppers. If you don't like a deal, you can just say "no."

QUALIFYING THE BUYER

If you're selling a computer yourself, you'll want to minimize the amount of time you waste on would-be buyers who have no idea what they want or need, on dreamers who fantasize about owning computers they can't afford, and on bargain hunters who want to steal your computer off your desk. Qualify buyers early in the game so that you can focus on people likely to sit down at the bargaining table and pass some cash. Buyer qualification entails a three-step process: finding out whether the buyer is looking for what you're offering, whether the buyer is serious, and what the buyer can afford.

Does the buyer want what you have?

To find out what the buyer really wants, you need to establish the buyer's level of computer literacy. If you were selling a car, you wouldn't be likely to get calls from people who ask what the steering wheel or the engine does. Computers have been around for far less time than cars, though, and to most of the world, VGA cards, 2-Meg SIMMs, I/O ports, and 387 coprocessor chips all sound like the parts list for NASA's lunar landing module.

Your job is to sell your machine, not teach Computing 101. Educating a naïve buyer is tantamount to free consulting. Besides, not only are you unlikely to make a sale (naïve would-be buyers scare easily), but in the event that you do, the new owner of your computer might rely on you as a tutor for life. We know of one poor soul who, after a year of late night questions about such arcana as the use of the DOS COPY command, finally got an unlisted number, at great inconvenience to his friends, family, and clients.

If a buyer asks any of the following questions, feign illness and wait for the next call.

- Does it have a typewriter part and a television part too?

- Is this the one my son saw on TV?

- What color is it? I'm looking for a computer that will go with my living room drapes.

Having established that you're not dealing with a novice, find out what the potential buyer intends to do with your equipment. If you're selling a 10-megabyte IBM XT or an Apple II and a buyer informs you that he or she wants to use it for heavy-duty desktop publishing or CAD applications, stop the negotiation. The transaction would come back to haunt you when the buyer discovered that he or she couldn't even install the software, let alone use it.

Even though, technically, you wouldn't have broken any laws, the buyer could make your life pretty miserable. Besides, if you were a buyer, wouldn't you be grateful if the seller of the machine you were salivating over said, "Gee, this computer just doesn't have the kind of horsepower you need to run that kind of software"? A bad match is simply not good business. Here are the essential questions to ask regarding the buyer's applications intentions:

- What software do you plan to use? What are its minimum hardware and memory requirements? If the buyer doesn't know and you aren't familiar with the software package, send the buyer back to do some homework. He or she can call the software publisher and find out if your hardware configuration will run the program adequately.

- What other programs do you expect to use in the next six months to a year? What are their requirements?

- What are your highest expansion plans for this system?

Be sure that your machine and the buyer's needs are a good match.

Sure, you can take advantage of an ignorant buyer, but that only generates bad karma, the kind that manifests itself as a glitch that vaporizes all the data on your new 300-megabyte hard disk. As the old saw says, What goes around comes around.

Is the buyer serious?

Many computer buyers do a lot of comparison shopping before making a decision. Some get stuck in eternal window-shopping mode, either because they don't have the wherewithal to buy a box of disks, let alone your system, or because they like to dream of owning a computer they have no real need for.

To separate the dreamers from the serious buyers, ask the following kinds of questions:

- How long do you plan to shop?

- When do you plan to make a decision?

- How soon do you need to be working with the computer?

- Does your purchase depend on the sale of something else?

- Are you really interested in buying my system? When can we get together to sign on the dotted line?

The most useful clue to a caller's seriousness is whether the potential buyer speaks as if he or she already owns the computer. Does the caller talk about what he or she will do with *your* computer, or *my* computer? The difference is subtle but significant. Someone who refers to the machine as "mine" is probably thinking seriously about owning it.

Can the buyer afford your machine?

No degree of persuasive selling will get a buyer to cough up more money than he or she has in the bank. If it's clear early in the conversation that the buyer is negotiating on a shoestring, cut the call and wait for a customer with means.

To identify the buyer who can afford your system, cut right to the chase. Simply ask, "Have you established a budget for the purchase of this computer?" If the answer is "Yes," proceed to establish the price. If the answer is "No," find out what the buyer intends to spend. If you can't get an answer, don't waste any more time.

Once you identify a suitable local buyer, be prepared to demo your machine.

STRUTTING YOUR STUFF

A sophisticated buyer who knows exactly what he or she needs—a Compaq Deskpro 286 with 1 megabyte of RAM and a 20-megabyte hard disk, say — generally won't ask you to demonstrate your computer's capabilities. But a prospective buyer with less computer experience might want to see exactly what your computer can do.

Use software that really shows off your machine's capabilities. A dazzling color graphics program always looks good. If you have a greased lightning hard disk, show its retrieval time with a database file. Whatever sold you on the system will probably get the buyer's blood pumping. Even if you are no longer enchanted with your machine's features or the manufacturer's canned demo, the buyer might find the features the demo shows off irresistible.

It's a good idea to run the application the buyer intends to use, too, or one close to it. Then the buyer can fairly determine whether the computer will meet his or her needs.

SELLING YOUR COMPUTER

Once you've found a qualified buyer who wants your machine, you can begin the process of reaching a mutually agreeable price. Before you start to deal, adopt the following strategic postures:

- Enter the negotiation from a position of strength and confidence. The buyer wants your computer; otherwise, you wouldn't be at the negotiation point.

- Acknowledge that you want to sell the computer. Your preferred outcome is the absence of the computer.

- Assume that the buyer is no fool. He or she will bring to the table his or her own strategies. Never underestimate a buyer when you're cutting a deal.

- Know ahead of time the price you'd like your machine to fetch and the price you'd accept.

Finally, never lose sight of the fact that you aren't out to recover your initial investment—you're looking for a fair deal. To guarantee your half of "fair," you need to know when to zig, when to zag, and when to zap the deal.

When to hold your ground

- The buyer wants the machine, the price is close, and the buyer came a long way to see it. Hold your own—he or she won't want to drive all the way back empty-handed. If you get stuck in a stalemate, at least get a phone number.

- The buyer's offer is too low. You have other possible buyers. Stand firm.

When to give in

- The offer is close to your asking price and at the top of the buyer's budget.

- You have an antique, and the buyer's doing you a favor to offer the price now on the table.

When to give up

- Buyers see the machine and shake their heads.

- Your asking price is down to 20 percent of your original purchase price, and that figure is still above the cost of a new clone.

- The buyer calculates the offer on a hand-held calculator that has more power than the computer you offer for sale.

We can't guarantee that every deal will go smoothly and yield the cash you believe you deserve, but if you play by the rules you'll maximize your chances for a fair deal. Above all, remember that computers are not only marvelous tools, they're *fun*. Selling your machine should be a pleasurable experience. If it's turning into an odious task, play the game with someone else.

STRATEGIES FOR BUYERS

Buyers who have never bought a used computer before often feel they're at the seller's mercy. That view simply doesn't hold up. If you're a qualified buyer, the seller needs you—he or she wants to make a deal and move on. After all, if the seller has already bought a new computer, the machine she still has to sell ties up her capital. If the seller can't buy a new computer until he finds a home for the current machine, the machine for sale is an impediment. As a buyer, you have a great deal of clout because you can decide who will be the recipient of your hard-earned cash. You can use that power to ensure that the result of the negotiation is a fair deal.

ACCOMMODATING YOUR SOFTWARE

You need to know your immediate goal in buying a computer and your ultimate objective. If you don't have a handle on what you need, you're more likely to spend too much on equipment you don't need or to go for a bargain on a system inadequate for your needs. If you don't know your ultimate objective, you'll quickly outgrow your new used machine.

Don't "wing it" when you pick up the phone to contact sellers. Meditate on your situation first. Ask yourself the following questions.

What software do I want to use on the computer today?

If you plan to use your existing software, be sure the machine you decide to look for has at least the capacity to run the software you use right now. If you plan to use new software, be sure you know the true power needs of the new package(s).

Software will function on the minimum hardware requirements listed by the manufacturer, but performance can be so slow that the software is almost useless. As a general rule, never settle for the minimum configuration. You'll often discover odd constraints that in aggregate compromise the program's full functioning.

What will my computing needs be in the future?

When we hear a buyer say, "Oh, I'll never need that much hard disk space or RAM," we shake our heads and smile. Just as work expands to fill the time allotted for it, information expands to fill the allotted space. (Coauthor Bennett reluctantly bought a 120-Meg hard disk when he upgraded his last computer, which had contained a 40-Meg hard disk. His colleagues urged him to buy the 120-Meg disk rather than the 60-Meg disk he originally intended to buy. After a year and a half, he found himself juggling 115 Megs of data!)

What fills up our hard disks? New software releases continually get bigger. Many word processing programs that once occupied fewer than 100,000 bytes now require two to four megabytes when fully configured with speller, hyphenation module, thesaurus, printer definition tables, printer and monitor drivers, and so on.

And software companies keep creating add-on and enhancements products for their packages. Individually, these programs might be relatively small, but together they chew up enormous amounts of disk space. If we have the space, we'll find a way to fill it up—it's just in our nature to do that.

Generally, the difference in cost between a 10-Meg hard disk machine and a 20-Meg hard disk machine, or between a 20-Meg hard disk machine and a 40-Meg hard disk machine, is small in proportion to the overall price. If your budget is so tight that all you can afford is a limited capacity disk, think about waiting a bit until you can afford to buy a higher capacity system for a slight increase in price. The more flexible you can be on price, the better your chances to take advantage of a real bargain.

What hardware will I need to add on in the future?

Will the machine you're buying take a hard disk, a second hard disk, memory expansion? Be sure you can add on to the computer you're thinking of buying.

What could I get new for the same money?

Know the best alternative to the purchase before you make a deal.

PRICING COMPUTERS

As a buyer, you start out with one asset: money. The best way to use that asset wisely is to consume information about the machine you want. Consult ads, used computer stores, brokerages, and several sellers of the same used equipment to get a fix on the price of a system that will meet your needs. The more you know about price, the better you will do when you negotiate a deal.

Be careful that you aren't comparing Apples and IBMs, systems from different eras, or brand names and clones. One potential customer of the Boston Computer Exchange wrote an irate letter asking how we could possibly list a used Compaq 386 system for sale at our price when he had seen an ad for a 386–based computer for one-third that price. "Brand new, brand spanking new," he wrote. This buyer didn't realize that he was comparing a cheap clone to state-of-the-art technology from one of the world's most innovative and reputable computer makers. If you don't know your pricing stuff, you'll waste everyone's time.

QUALIFYING THE SELLER

Just as sellers must screen time-wasting buyers, buyers must pinpoint sellers who have exactly what they want. This involves several inquiries: finding out exactly what the seller has to offer, determining the condition of the equipment, finding out why the seller wants to sell, and getting a sense of the seller's target price. Let's take a closer look at each question.

Does the seller have what I want?

Very few systems retain their basic configuration systems because users constantly add bells and whistles. Given the inevitable customizations, the buyer must ask, "Is the machine a reasonable facsimile of what I want?" Discount all the frills you don't need. Maybe you want a Macintosh SE with 1 megabyte of RAM and the seller has one with 2.5 megabytes. Do you care about the extra memory? Is it worth anything to you? If not, negotiate it out of the deal. In any case, no little "extras" should sway your thinking. Buy what you need now and in the reasonable future, and consider the rest "freebies" the seller tosses in to sweeten the deal.

Does the seller's machine work?

Answer this question at the outset. If anything in the system works intermittently or is broken, you're generally better off going on to the next seller instead of knocking bucks off the price. (Refer to Chapter 5 for a detailed discussion of testing used computer equipment.) It's rarely worth the time and hassle to fix equipment unless you happen to have the parts handy and can drop them into the box with a minimum of effort. Your mission is to buy a computer, not to salvage one.

Why is the seller selling?

Every seller has a reason for trying to move his or her computer. The more you know about the seller's motivation, the better you can judge his or her willingness to negotiate to a lower price. The seller's reason for selling might be irrelevant to you, but his or her need to sell can become your opportunity. If the computer doesn't have enough expansion slots for all the cards the seller needs to use, you, too, might lament the machine's limited expansion capabilities. And we've heard of many great deals in which the seller needed cash in a hurry and his or her desperation became a buyer's bonanza. Find out why the seller is selling, and act accordingly.

What price does the seller hope to get?

The simple question, "What kind of money are you looking for?" will tell you whether the seller is acting out fantasies or is in touch with the marketplace. If the seller tries to tell you the machine is worth 90 percent of its original value even though it's been supplanted by three generations of newer models, you must decide whether it's worth your while to educate the seller or better to move on. Your tolerance should last about five minutes: If the seller won't acknowledge the existence of a notion called "fair market value," keep dialing. And remember that a neutral valuation from an outside party can help get a negotiation on track.

Buying the Computer

As we've stressed, you have a lot more clout than buyers often think they do. Approach the deal methodically and with a cool head. Keep the nuts-and-bolts issues in mind when you sit down at the negotiating table.

When to hold your ground

- You know how much money the seller needs to get for the computer.
- Your offer is fair, and other sellers are available.

When to give in

- You really need the equipment, and the seller's price is close to the amount you've budgeted.
- The seller still needs the equipment and hesitates to deliver the equipment immediately, but you need it now and other sellers aren't readily available to you.

When to give up

- The asking price is fair, but you simply can't afford that kind of money.
- Demand for the equipment is strong, and you know other buyers are willing to pay the asking price.

There are enough used computers sitting around to satisfy every (reasonable) buyer in the secondary market. If you start off with the right mind-set and observe the rules, you're likely to find the machine you're looking for at a price you can afford.

Universal Rules of Negotiation

The following general rules apply to any transaction in the secondary computer market:

- Get reliable price data from a neutral party before you enter into a negotiation.

- Verify that the seller wants to sell and that the buyer wants to buy to ensure that you don't waste time with a nonplayer.

- Know the best alternative to the deal. Would you be able to sell your computer if this deal fell through? Could you find another machine if you couldn't reach an agreement? Know your alternatives so that you can enter the negotiation unemotionally.

- Don't bluff or lie. The secondary computer market is strewn with deals that went sour because the seller, the buyer, or both bluffed in hopes of a fantasy outcome.

- Approach the negotiation with a win-win attitude. If you do it right, the seller moves what he or she doesn't want and the buyer gets what he or she is seeking.

Randall's Rules

- The more time it takes to close a deal, the greater the chances the deal will fall through or that someone will decide he or she is getting screwed.

- Sellers, remember that buyers are looking at your computer and at lots of others.

- Buyers, remember that the seller wants to move the equipment today.

CHAPTER 7

SIGNED, SEALED, AND DELIVERED

Engaging in Safe Sales

❖❖

Randall's Notebook

October 15–16, 1988

Boston, Massachusetts

❖❖

10:00 A.M. A woman calls from outside New Haven, Connecticut, wanting to sell a Macintosh II her uncle has given her. John, a new broker at the Exchange, tells her that $4,000 would be a fair asking price. The seller says, "OK."

11:00 A.M. John asks Joyce, the sales manager, to approve the new listing before it's processed into the database. Flabbergasted, Joyce tells him the price is ludicrous. "Three thousand, tops, absolute tops," she says, shaking her head.

11:15 A.M. John sheepishly calls the seller back, expecting to get his shorts blown off. To his surprise, the seller says, "Three thousand? Fine."

11:45 A.M. John calls several buyers and within an hour makes a sale. The buyer, who lives in New Haven, wires funds to us and picks up the machine from the seller.

3:00 P.M. The buyer calls the Exchange to tell us that the computer doesn't seem to have any serial numbers. We tell him to open the cover and tell us what's inside. He reports a highly unusual apparatus, an analog/digital converter board, which does have a serial number.

3:30 P.M. We call the A/D board maker, who informs us that the serial number is registered to Yale University.

3:45 P.M. We call the Yale University police and ask whether any Macintosh IIs are missing. The sergeant says he'll check and call us back tomorrow.

The next morning. Two serious looking guys in sunglasses and trench coats come to the door. They flash FBI badges. They want to know about our "fencing operation." Four hundred computers have disappeared from the Yale area, and the FBI thinks we're dispensing the stolen merchandise. Five grueling hours of questioning later, the G-men leave, satisfied that we're legit. So much for being a good citizen.

Epilogue. After apprehending, trying, and convicting the interstate theft suspects, the FBI staffers call to ask whether they can get a good price on computers for their desks: "Now that Gramm-Rudman effectively limits our department to no more than a thousand dollars per computer, we were wondering if you could get us some...." We help the crime fighters upgrade to better computers. Now that's being a good citizen.

➨

HOT COMPUTERS

Had John been an experienced broker, his sixth-sense burglar alarm would have gone off when the seller agreed to a $1,000 price drop without so much as a peep. That's a good sign that a machine is hot. Since the Boston Computer Exchange opened for business in 1982, at least 50 thieves have tried to sell other people's computers through our services. In each case, the *modus operandi* has been nearly the same. The seller wanted cash immediately. The seller had no information about the computer. The seller had a thin story about how he got the machine. And the seller balked at requests for documentation, invoices, or any other paperwork.

Stolen goods are only one hazard of dealing in the secondary market. A buyer might write a bogus check or a seller never ship the goods. A seller might try to pawn off broken gear or a buyer try to return a broken computer (not the one she bought).

Early in the history of the Exchange, a customer bought a pallet of used XTs from a seemingly reputable company. The boxes that reached him were labeled IBM but contained old phone books. For us, that was the end of the honor system. A month later we instituted our escrow system, in which we hold the buyer's money until the seller has delivered working goods. Sadly, we've become policemen as well as computer brokers.

We don't want to imply that the secondary computer market is a dangerous place to plunk down your money, but we do want you to exercise common sense before you make a move that might cost you your gear or leave a hole in your bank account.

TO CATCH A THIEF

Most used computers are bought and sold legitimately, but the world has its share of thieves, and as high ticket, portable items, computers are easy pickin's. Other than a seller's running off with your money, the worst fate that can befall you is to buy a stolen computer. When you buy through a store, a broker, a liquidator, or a reputable mail-order company, you can usually rest assured that the intermediary

Profile of a Thief

How do you know whether you're dealing with a thief? Here are some general guidelines. (The thief described in Randall's Notebook exhibited two of these traits.)

→ The seller received the computer from an "uncle" and has no use for it. (For some reason uncles seem to be the relatives of choice as opposed to grandmothers or sisters.) "Uncle" gave the machine to the seller, so she doesn't know much about it.

→ The seller will accept any offer for the machine without putting up a fight. A thief doesn't care about fair market value and will take whatever he can get. Given his cost of goods, it's all gravy.

→ The seller doesn't have any paperwork. "Uncle didn't give me any receipt or other paperwork. I can't call him now to get the papers—he doesn't have a telephone." The harder you press for details about "Uncle," the more fictitious he sounds.

→ The machine is missing some essential component, and the seller doesn't seem to understand that the machine is incomplete. The most common missing components are keyboards and keyboard cords, AC cords, and documentation. Thieves frequently overlook these components in their haste to get stolen goods out the door.

has checked out ownership and taken legitimate title to the computer before selling it to you.

If you're buying a computer on your own, you'll need to do a little

- ➺ The seller isn't disturbed by, or doesn't have any explanation for, the fact that cables from the various ports have been either ripped off or sliced with a wire cutter. Treat any evidence of quick and violent disassembly with caution. People who own computers generally treat them with kid gloves.

- ➺ The seller can't explain why there aren't any serial numbers on the machines. "Gee, how about that! I guess my uncle took them off for safekeeping or something. I didn't know these things ate cereal."

- ➺ The seller refuses to meet at a respectable place. The Exchange actually received a call from someone who wanted to sell us a computer from the trunk of his car!

- ➺ The seller doesn't know anything about the system. If the seller draws a blank when you use the words "RAM," "disk drives," and "ports" or when you ask questions about model names, beware. Even a new user should have some familiarity with the basic terms of the trade.

- ➺ The seller refuses to let you test the equipment. Thieves are uneasy and get nervous when you question the state of the equipment. They tend to get worried if you do anything that stretches out the sale. "Hey, Man, I gotta catch a bus so I can visit my sick aunt at the nursing home."

legwork yourself. The burden is on you to ensure that the person selling the machine actually owns it or is fully authorized to sell it.

What proves ownership? Ultimately, the serial number on a piece of paper—a bill of sale, a dealer's invoice, or an original receipt from a seller. Some dealers don't put the serial number on the original invoice, so a plausible invoice from an original source is the best you can get from some sellers. Yes, anyone with a desktop publishing program can fake an invoice or a bill of sale, but most computer thieves aren't that smart. They seldom know enough about the machines they steal to be able to turn them on, let alone navigate DOS or create a PageMaker layout.

It all comes down to good judgment. A *bona fide* owner won't object to a little probing into the legal status of a machine. A *bona fide* owner won't object if you ask to see an invoice, a bill of sale, or other original paperwork. A thief will object to anything other than a fast cash sale.

TO VERIFY THAT THE MACHINE IS HOT

Unfortunately, there are few avenues for tracing the ownership of a machine. You can call the National Association of Computer Dealers Hotline (see the resource list in Appendix B), but you can't depend on their information to be complete. Manufacturers generally don't keep lists of stolen machines; neither do the police nor the FBI.

If you do suspect that the computer you're offered is stolen, get as much information about the seller as possible, postpone the deal, and contact the local authorities. If you have carted home what turns out to be a stolen computer, you should contact the police because they might want the machine as evidence. The original victim might have posted a reward. Let your conscience be your guide.

GETTING WHAT YOU PAID FOR

Sometimes a buyer sends a seller money and never sees a computer in return. You won't have this problem if you deal with a legitimate store, broker, or liquidator. If you buy at a store or from a liquidator, you walk away with your computer after you pay for it. If you buy through a broker, your payment will be held in escrow until you have a working machine in hand. If you buy long-distance from a private party or even a company, be prepared for possible rip-offs.

Obviously, sending money to a distant address listed in a classified ad is a dicey proposition. The risk is greatest if you buy from an individual. If you buy from an out-of-town company, use a national credit card for payment. If you pay with a major national credit card and never receive the machine or find that the machine has been misrepresented to you and the vendor is unwilling to make good on what he promised, you can call in and have the payment cancelled. If the company doesn't have a national reputation or take credit cards, think twice about doing business with it.

WARRANTIES AND SERVICE CONTRACTS

If you buy a used computer from a store, you might get a 30-day warranty. If you buy from a retailer or used computer store, the outfit owes you some assurance that the computer will work.

How important is the presence or absence of a warranty? Not very. The chances are excellent that if a computer works when you turn it on, it will work 30 days later. Computers tend either to fail the first time they are turned on or to last for years. Of course, you might buy a machine that has lasted for years but that dies a natural death 29 days after you sign the papers. In that unlikely case, a 30-day warranty will save your neck. But odds are that if the machine works when you buy it, it will last well beyond the period for which any sane seller would warrant the goods.

Buyers tend to regard warranties as great assurance against bad equipment. What you really need is assurance that a machine will operate the first time you flip the power switch. It should be some comfort to you to know that a seller can't pour the

Checking Out a Warranty

➥ Is the warranty a "depot" type in which you take the machine to the store for repair or an "on-site" type in which the store sends someone to your home or office to solve the problem on the spot? The more expensive on-site warranties are usually limited to transactions within a local area. Some national companies (IBM, Sorbus, TRW, and others) offer on-site maintenance contracts regardless of the age of the computer. You can arrange with IBM, for example, to have a technician test your computer at your home or office. If the computer passes their tests, IBM will write a maintenance contract, with no charge for the visit. If you decide against the maintenance contract, you'll be charged for the testing time.

On-site maintenance contracts are pricey because they reflect the travel costs of the technician (the "portal-to-portal" fee) as well as the cost of parts and the "service" itself.

➥ What does the warranty cover? The most expensive components in a computer are generally the hard disk and the motherboard, but add-on boards and high-end monitors can be costly to repair or replace, too. IBM's PS/2 computers with the Micro Channel Architecture equivalent of sawdust into the "transmission" to make a bad computer stagger through a test run, only to fail a few hours later. In the vast majority of transactions we've brokered through the Exchange, the buyer has been able to run the equipment right out of the box, and it still ran more than 30 days later. In the few cases in which the equipment did fail, the problems were inexpensive and easy to

(Models 50 and up), for instance, offer a mixed advantage in that they combine most components on the motherboard. On the positive side, everything is compactly mounted on one board. On the negative side, if one component goes, you usually need to replace the entire board. At the time of this writing, the motherboard for a PS/2 Model 70 lists at a staggering $3,995. (The company will sell you a refurbished motherboard for about $1,000 plus your old board.) The moral? A warranty for a PS/2 would be worthless if it didn't cover replacement of the motherboard.

→ Is the party qualified to fix the computer? If you buy a Macintosh from a resale store whose stock is 99 percent IBM machines, ask how they plan to honor the Mac's warranty. Many used computer stores are great at servicing one brand of machine but have limited capability to service anything else. If the store seems to sell at least one of everything, ask where they'd do the service work on your computer. If it's a tiny shop and they say, "We have factory-trained service personnel for all major computer makes," shop elsewhere. It is nearly impossible for one tiny store to payroll factory-trained personnel for all of *anything* in the computer field.

remedy. If a service contract is important to you, you can usually buy one from a party other than the seller, so don't pass up a good deal because of a warranty or service contract issue.

Stores generally provide warranties with the sale of used machines. Read the warranty carefully to find out whether it's appropriate for the computer you're buying.

If you have an option to buy an extended service contract, don't. By and large, whatever it will cost you to get a machine fixed will be less than the cost of the extended contract. (An exception, of course, is the extended warranty on IBM PS/2 Models 50 and up, given the high cost of replacing their motherboards.)

Some outfits make the argument that you need a service contract to get a critical computer back on line in the event of a disaster. In our experience, the best way to cover a critical computer is to have a low-cost replacement system that can be pressed into service or cannibalized in a pinch. Or have a stock of critical parts on hand at all times. Both are expensive, you say? That depends on the cost to you of downtime. If your business absolutely depends on a functioning computer at all times, a service contract wouldn't be enough, anyway. Consider keeping a complete backup computer system that mirrors all the data on your critical system—just in case.

GETTING THE MONEY

The major pitfall for the seller in a transaction is getting the money. If you deal directly with a buyer, especially a long-distance buyer, don't send your computer into the twilight zone without getting payment first.

Regardless of the distance involved, unless you know the person or company, accept only a cashier's check, a money order, a certified check, or cash. The seller can hand you a rubber check personally just as easily as he can pop one into the mailbox.

Brokers or other intermediaries that escrow money make transactions safer. The escrow system ensures both that the buyer receives working goods and that the funds are good.

If you do decide to handle your own transaction, be aware that the buyer can stop check and credit card payments. The buyer can even stop payment on a certified check, in a pinch. You're better off insisting on cash, a money order, or a cashier's check, or that the buyer send payment by wire. For a big transaction, it's a good idea to ask for an irrevocable letter of credit.

No form of payment is foolproof—not even a money order. We learned that the hard way. In 1985, a customer bought $900 worth of components from us with a bogus money order. When we called the bank, the officer told us they were having a lot of trouble with phony money orders. That was too bad for us because the bank wouldn't honor the money order. And it was too bad for the thief. A year later I took the forger to court. She pleaded guilty to the charges and was sentenced to a stint in the state penitentiary. But we lost the money and our computer gear.

If you take a personal check, you run the risk of getting burned. The buyer might stop payment or have insufficient funds in his bank account. To gain a measure of security, call the bank to be sure it exists and ask the bank to verify that the account has sufficient funds to cover the check. This precautionary measure isn't foolproof—the buyer might have hundreds of outstanding checks or plan to stop payment—but it does offer some peace of mind.

RESOLVING THE STALEMATE

By now, you might have noticed a potential standoff in transacting for a computer: If both parties carried our advice to its logical conclusions, sellers wouldn't ship anything until the cash was in, and buyers wouldn't send off their money until they received working machines. One solution to the impasse is simple. If you're going to do your own deal, avoid long-distance transactions. Do the deal face-to-face. The buyer should test the equipment on the spot, and the seller should insist on cash or a money order. For long-distance deals, use the services of a broker or another neutral party.

LEGAL ISSUES

A "neat" sale ties up all the loose ends and doesn't neglect the interests of software companies or the state.

SELLING OR DONATING SOFTWARE

Used computer sales often raise the issue of accompanying software. Most computer owners don't realize that they don't really own software they've bought. They own the media (disks) on which the software resides, but they license from the software publisher the right to use the program's code. Licensing agreements vary by publisher, but unless you license a network version of the software, the common understanding is that you cannot use the software on more than one machine at the same time.

Single-user licensing agreements
When you sell or donate software, the licensing issue comes into play. Microsoft, for example, does not restrict your transferring software license rights to someone else for cash or for free—*provided that you do not keep any copies of the program.*

Site licensing requirements
Many software publishers sell site licenses that allow the buyer, who pays a flat fee, to use the software simultaneously on as many machines as are designated by the licensing agreement. If you have a site license, you need to check with the publisher before you sell or give away the program.

Prior releases

Under many licensing agreements, it is illegal to sell prior releases of a program. If you *upgrade* from Microsoft Word 4.0 to Word 5.0, for example, Microsoft requires that you destroy your 4.0 disks and remove 4.0 from your computer. In other words, you cannot use version 5.0 yourself and sell version 4.0 to someone else. Even though the versions are significantly different, the fact that they're versions of the same software program means that two machines would be using the program at the same time, which violates the basic licensing agreement.

If you *buy* a copy of Word 5.0 outright, rather than through an upgrade program, you are free to sell your version 4.0 as long as you destroy any backup copies.

The Seller's Responsibilities

All of this bears heavily on the seller of a used computer, especially of a computer that has a hard disk. If you do not remove licensed application programs from your hard disk before you transfer your computer to a new owner and you continue to use the same software after copying it onto your new machine, you're probably breaking the law. Unless you explicitly sell the software and the buyer accepts the terms of the end user license agreement that governs use of the software and you plan to destroy all copies at your own site, be sure that your hard disk is clean.

Even if you legally sell or give away a software program, you will still be considered the registered user in the eyes of the publisher. The new owner or recipient of the software will not receive automatic upgrade notices, will not be entitled to upgrade discounts, and might not be able to receive technical support. Transfer the software registration to the new owner.

Transferring software registration is usually a simple matter. Some publishers will transfer the registration in response to your telephoned request. Others, such as Microsoft, require you to write a letter stating that you have sold or given away the software, have destroyed all backup copies, and have designated a specified individual as the new owner. From that point on, the company will consider the copy of the software to be registered in the new owner's name. The sample memo shown in Figure 7-1 gives you an idea of how to proceed.

To: Upgrade/registration department

Fr:

Re: Transfer of registration for [software name]

This letter is to inform you that I have transferred the license rights of my copy of [software program name] [version #], [serial # if available] to [new owner's name, address, city, state, phone]. [New owner's name] agrees to abide by the end user license governing the software. I have destroyed all backup copies of [software program name] and have removed the program from my hard disk. Please transfer the registration to [new owner's name].

Thank you for your attention to this matter.

_____

Former Owner

_____

New Owner

Figure 7-1.
A simple memo like the one shown here will take care of transferring your software license rights to a new owner.

SALES TAXES AND USE TAXES

Sales taxes on used computers is a thorny issue, and taxes vary from state to state, country to country. In most states, the transaction between two individuals for a used computer is treated as a casual sale and is not subject to tax. Check out the requirements in your state. If you make it a practice to trade in the used computer marketplace, you are no longer making casual sales and you'd better take care of your legal responsibilities.

If you buy a computer out of state from a used computer store, liquidator, or broker, you still might not be home free from the tax standpoint. In many states, the buyer is subject to a "use tax" on all goods purchased from any source. The buyer is required to pay the use tax, just as he or she would pay a sales tax on a taxable item. A buyer who lives in a state that levies a use tax must pay the tax money to the state taxing agency.

TRANSFER DOCUMENTS

If you are doing a sale on your own, several documents can enhance the safety of the transaction. The seller should be willing to issue the buyer a bill of sale and a receipt of funds. The buyer should be willing to issue a receipt of goods. A single form like the one shown in Figure 7-2 on the next page should cover it all, and a copy to each party should take care of the paperwork. Run the sample by your attorney before you use it, especially if you are trading goods under unusual circumstances.

A transfer document completes the transaction: It lays out the terms of the sale and the item(s) traded, clarifies the title to the goods, and proves that the transaction has occurred. Be sure that you list all equipment normally sold as single units, especially expansion boards, and that you record all serial numbers. If the seller has maintained an equipment log such as the one we show in Chapter 9, filling out a transfer document should be easy.

Provide two copies of the document—one for each party—and you're in business!

Bill of Sale

This record of transaction is made on the _____ day of _____ , 19 _____

from _____ (the "Seller")

to _____ (the "Buyer").

The Seller has agreed to sell and the buyer has agreed to purchase the following equipment:

_____

_____

_____

_____

_____ (the "Property").

The Seller warrants that the Seller has clear title to and ownership of the Property in its entirety and that the Property is not otherwise encumbered. The Seller warrants that it is in the Seller's sole discretion to sell the Property as per this receipt. The Seller warrants that the Property is fully operational and contains no defects except those listed below:

_____

_____

_____

The Seller has agreed to accept, and the buyer has agreed to pay, the sale price of $_____ .

By so signing, the Seller agrees that title to these goods is transferred to the Buyer and that the Seller has received good funds in the amount stated herein and that this transcation is hereby closed.

Seller: _____

Buyer: _____

Date: _____

Figure 7-2.
A bill of sale like the one shown here covers all the bases.

Randall's Rules

➻ Don't trust strangers. Everyone's a stranger, and some are stranger than others.

➻ When a man says he's honest, hold on to your wallet or your computer.

➻ If your check is in the mail, my computer isn't.

➻ If your computer's in the mail, my check will follow— after I receive the computer and test it.

CHAPTER 8

WRAPPING
IT UP

Cleaning and Shipping Your Computer

➤◄

Randall's Notebook
March 19, 1985
Boston, Massachusetts

➤◄

UPS delivers a tired looking box bearing the ghost of an IBM logo. The patchwork tape and crumpled corners make me nervous. The only thing worse than seeing a computer arrive in a Chiquita banana box sealed with duct tape and twine is to get one shipped in its original carton for the thirty-fifth time. The tape strata betray the box's shipping history, and the crumpled corners suggest that the machine inside has been dropped by the shippers as many times as new tape has been laid down.

Peeling off the shipping labels is like doing an archaeological dig. Each layer reveals a piece of history. It's a litany of buyers and sellers. Chances are excellent that the machine is a dog in search of a pound.

Surprisingly, the IBM AT we uncrate is in pretty good shape. No boot-up problems, and despite a collection of dust and some minor grime under the hood, it's perfectly operable. After a once-over with Windex and the vacuum cleaner, I take a look at the hard disk. To my surprise, it's full!

And what an assortment of goodies. The spreadsheets trace the demise of the owner's company from financially troubled to foreclosure and Chapter 11. Pretty entertaining, but not as much fun as the assortment of business letters in the word processing directory. The really juicy stuff, though, is buried in a subdirectory of love letters to the owner's girlfriend. Not only has this anti-Trump lost his business, but his love affair has cost him his marriage, and the details of the divorce are messy.

The cleansing power of the FORMAT command washes the disk clean and with it the secrets of the Casanova who's failed to purge his computer before shipping it out the door. As I rebox the machine, I get an idea for a novel about an owner of a used computer store who develops a multimillion dollar blackmail operation based on embarrassing data left on hard disks. Nah, who would believe it?

❧

THE RESPONSIBLE SELLER

The owner of the IBM AT with the scandalous spreadsheets and the lurid love letters was lucky—his secrets never passed beyond the eyes of a discreet viewer. But the seller is responsible for making sure that the computer is ready for market. This will require some time, but in the end it's worth it—you'll get the fewest complaints from your buyer and avoid disasters that can nix a deal, cost you your machine, or put you in an embarrassing situation. The various types of necessary preparations are described below, and you'll find a checklist in this chapter to help you be sure your computer is ready for market.

REMOVING SOFTWARE AND DATA

To be safe, remove *all* files from your hard disk. If you are not selling the operating system with the computer, remove its files as well. Note that the sale (or gift) of an operating system is governed by the same conditions we described for software applications in Chapter 7. If you haven't bought a new, separate, copy of the software, you don't have the right to either sell or give away the copy on the computer you are selling unless you keep no copy for your own use. If you leave either your operating system software or your application programs on the hard disk and simply pass them on to someone else, you'll break the law by illegally distributing copyrighted software. (See the discussion of transferring software license rights in Chapter 7.) And you certainly don't want to pass confidential or personal data on to a stranger. Be smart and safe. Clean the disk. Completely.

Transfer your software and data to another machine or archive it before you clean your hard disk. You might need deinstallation "keys" to remove some program files from a hard disk. (Older versions of Lotus 1-2-3, dBASE, Framework, and others work this way.) Deinstallation keys reside on your original distribution disks. Most software publishers gave up on such copy protection schemes in the late 1980s, but check your manuals if you are not sure whether your programs require special deinstallation procedures.

To transfer program and data files from the computer you plan to sell, you have several options:

- Move your files manually to floppies using a copy command. You can copy the software to another computer later. This is the slowest method and the one with which you're most prone to lose files through haste and bad calls—"Was XTKDFS.Z43 a critical operating file, or just some junk?"

- Use a backup program (such as Fastback Plus for DOS machines or HD Backup for the Macintosh) to cram more data onto fewer disks. You'll need to buy the backup program, but this method is cost effective and fast. To restore the files, you'll need to install the backup software in your new machine.

- Download the data onto a tape drive system. This is the most expensive option, but if you have lots of data that should be backed up regularly anyway, a tape drive will turn out to be a good one-time investment.

- Move the data from your old computer to your new computer with a direct cable and transfer software. Products such as the Brooklyn Bridge, LapLink, and FastWire move data from PC to PC at an astounding rate. This is the fastest method, and it's relatively inexpensive. But it also requires that you keep your old computer until you've bought your new one and have transferred the data. This might not be logistically or economically feasible for you.

After you've moved the data to floppies, tape, or another computer, erase the files or format the hard disk with the appropriate operating system command. This will make the disk look clean to the casual observer, but be aware that erasing files or formatting a disk does *not* make the files irretrievable. The Norton and Mace utilities for MS-DOS–based machines, for example, each contain a utility for unerasing files, or even unformatting hard disks—a blessing for the clumsy typist but a potential problem for anyone trying to hide confidential data.

If you want to be really sure that your disk is data free, use a program such as the Norton utility WIPEDISK, which replaces all information with a zero or another character you specify. Then the files can't be unerased (at least not with most commercially available software utilities).

Do you need to go to the extent of using special programs to hide your data? That depends. If your computer contains the formula for an unpatented elixir of life, you'd better be sure it's irretrievable. But if your disk contains your bowling league spreadsheet or Italian recipes, don't waste your time or money. Unless you have a proprietary white sauce, just erase the files and clean up the computer's exterior—which brings us to the next point.

SPRUCING UP YOUR COMPUTER

What does it take to clean a computer? The same thing it takes to clean your bathroom. You don't need to buy special monitor glass spray cleaners or wipes. They're generally overpriced reformulations of conventional cleaning products. And for goodness sake, don't run out and buy an expensive "special computer vacuum" or "computer cleaning kit." In the same way that an auto care products industry, with an array of "special" interior seat and dashboard cleaners and rug shampoos, has grown up, the PC revolution has spawned a variety of old products with new names, at premium prices. (One of our favorites is the "special" felt tipped pen suited for writing on disk labels. What felt tip pen isn't?) Here's what you actually need:

    1 spray bottle of glass cleaner
    1 soft, lint free rag, preferably an old cotton T-shirt
        or cotton sock
    1 vacuum cleaner with a crevice attachment

To clean the machine, first turn the power off and unplug it. Then start at the top:

1. Vacuum dust and lint from the monitor vents. (You should do this periodically anyway, to ensure good air flow.)

2. Clean the monitor glass.

3. Wipe down the monitor case with a slightly moist rag. If you've had tape on the monitor, rub the spot with a little glass cleaner. If that doesn't do it, try lighter fluid or VM&P naphtha. You might have to resort to nail polish remover (acetone) to remove the glue, but that might stain the plastic—acetone will strip anything from the case, including paint. (It's better to keep stickers off your monitor from the start than to try to take them off later.) Regardless of the cleaners you deploy, apply them with common sense; like cats, computers don't like to be bathed.

4. Clean the case of the CPU. Vacuum the air vents. If you are comfortable opening the hood, do so and *carefully* vacuum the inside. (You'll be amazed at what can accumulate in a computer. Coauthor Randall once forgot to replace a slot cover on his AT after removing a defective memory board. Several days later, his machine was plagued by odd glitches. He lifted the hood to discover that his computer had become the outhouse of choice for the mice in his building and—not known to modern science before this—that mouse droppings are electrically conductive. A quick vacuuming job, and the computer was as good as new.)

   If you do vacuum your PC, be sure not to touch the nozzle to the boards or chips—you can break a solder connection or damage a component. Note that, particularly in winter, the vacuum nozzle can develop a high static-electricity charge, which can spell disaster to memory and some internal components. Be careful.

5. Clean the keyboard with a moist rag or a dab of spray cleaner applied to the rag. Do *not* spray the keys! Keyboards take a lot of abuse—thousands of hours of contact with sweat and oils from human fingers. Unfortunately, more than anything else, the cleanliness of a keyboard governs the buyer's perception of a used computer's condition. Although such thoroughness usually isn't necessary, you can pry off the keys on many keyboards and vacuum underneath them. (Check with the manufacturer first!) Always remove keyboard helper decals—they tend to reinforce the perception that the machine is secondhand.

GATHERING UP THE SMALL STUFF

Once the machine is spanking clean, the next step is to collect the manuals, the cables, and any other small parts that were originally supplied with the computer. The manuals are important; many people feel that the sale is incomplete without them, even if they never open the covers. You should ship the manual and the cables with the CPU, as the manufacturer packaged them originally. Now let's talk about packing up the machine.

BRACING YOUR MACHINE FOR THE HAUL

Whether your computer will travel cross-town in the trunk of someone's car or cross-country in the cargo bay of a 747, you must make every possible effort to ensure that it arrives intact. Computers generally suffer two types of damage while in transit: internal damage because boards are loose or hard drive heads haven't been "parked" (locked in place) and external damage from rough handling. You can prevent both types.

Internal Havoc

The single greatest cause of "dead-on-arrival" machines is poor packing. All too frequently a seller takes a perfectly good computer, packs it in a thin layer of paper, peanuts, or hard foam chunks, and sends it out on the road. You can avoid most internal damage by making sure that all boards and disk drives are tightly secured in place. A loose board can bend or even break a connecting pin. If a board should wiggle free, it might damage not only itself but a board nearby.

If the heads on a hard drive haven't been parked, they can vibrate while traveling and damage the drive medium. Many new computers have hard disks that automatically park the heads each time the computer is shut off. Older computers usually come with a program that will allow you to park the heads through a software command. Either way, be sure the heads are parked before you proceed.

Another way to minimize internal damage is to put any of the original shipping devices supplied by the manufacturer into the box. (We hope you've saved them.) The original Compaq Deskpro, for example, was shipped with a special pin that locked the hard disk in a parked position. Many computers come with cardboard disk inserts that minimize the chance of floppy drive damage during transport. Put cardboard inserts or "scratch" disks into each floppy drive and close the drive doors.

Printers usually come with special packaging devices, too. Most dot matrix printers have a special piece of hard foam or cardboard or a tieback to keep the print head from sliding back and forth. Laser printers often have shipping restraints to keep the fusor roller from turning and the mirror assembly from bouncing around and getting out of alignment. Keep this stuff, and use it. If you trashed the packaging when you opened the box, improvise, take your chances with shippers, or sell locally to a buyer who can pick up the gear and assume responsibility for getting it home intact.

External Damage

Your best protection against rough handling is a strong packaging defense. Ideally, you'll still have the original shipping cartons and the contoured plastic shells and foam pads that held the machine snugly in place. If you don't have them, fashion your own—just because a package is marked "fragile" doesn't mean that shippers will treat it gently. (The "fragile" marker seems to invite the opposite behavior.)

If you do make your own packaging, here are some guidelines:

- Never use crumpled newspaper for any part of the packaging.

- Never count on a loose "moat" of plastic peanuts alone to secure the machine. And don't wrap a machine in chunks of foam from some other product and stuff it into the wrong size box—an invitation to disaster. Instead, wrap at least two layers of plastic bubble sheeting around the machine itself. Seal the corners of the sheeting with tape and be sure there are no uncovered projections. Ensure that there are no openings through which packing material can invade the computer. Then place the bubble-wrapped machine in a bed of solid foam in a box significantly larger than the machine. Fill the sides and top of the box with solid foam to make a snug fit. Don't forget to put foam on top of the wrapped machine. The machine might be turned over in shipping and damaged by direct contact with the inside top of the box. A solid fill of plastic peanuts won't do it. The safest approach is to use sheets of foam rubber.

- *Never, never* use a box that is just "a bit larger" than the computer—you won't be able to cram enough packing material into the space between the box and the PC. Use a box that is at least six inches longer, wider, and higher on each side than the wrapped machine. (See Figure 8-1 on the next page.)

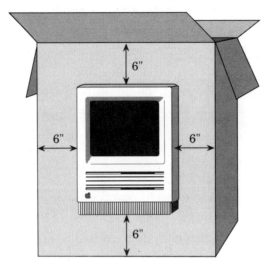

Figure 8-1.
*The box should allow plenty of room for
plastic bubble sheeting and foam.*

Tears come to our eyes at the memory of two Compaq portables that reached a buyer D.O.A. because their owner packed them side by side in a box a fraction of an inch larger than the combined volume of the machines. With no cushioning material at all, the computers took every drop, bump, and vibration as a direct hit. The buyer reported that when he took them out of the box, they looked as if they'd been air dropped to his office—without a parachute. The buyer got a 100 percent refund, and the seller got back a box of Compaq shrapnel.

The best course of action is keep the original packaging. Don't ever get lulled into thinking you can trash your box and packaging because you'll keep the machine forever—odds are, you won't. Without the original box and packing material, you're in for hassle and anxiety. Save the box and spare yourself unnecessary grief.

Wrapping It Up Checklist

→ Back up or transfer your software and data.

→ Deinstall your software.

→ Format and wipe your hard disk.

→ Park your hard disk head (if your disk drive isn't self-parking).

→ Remove the components you aren't selling.

→ Clean the monitor, case, and keyboard.

→ Vacuum the interior.

→ Secure the interior components:

☐ Tighten add-in boards in place.

☐ Insert cardboard floppy disk spacers in the drives.

☐ Close the floppy drive doors.

☐ Restrain the printer heads and all other movable components.

→ Gather up all the subcomponents (manuals, cables, small parts).

→ Pack the machine securely, and insure it.

Choosing a Carrier

The name of the game is accountability. You want a shipper who will produce a signature at the end. This might be your only proof that what you sent got to its destination. Never ship a machine via the US Mail—you'll have no way to prove that the computer actually reached the buyer. For cross-town deliveries, taxicabs and private couriers are a good idea, especially if you plead with the driver not to use your delivery for his Indianapolis 500 training. You can send a receipt-of-goods document along with the computer and have the driver return it to you.

UPS and Federal Express, Airborne, and the other courier services are all excellent means of shipping computer equipment out of town. They all offer insurance at a reasonable cost. Never forgo the insurance—a penny saved is often a kilobuck burned. Insurance will cover their failure to deliver, loss of the package, and negligent handling, but it won't cover your bad packing, an incorrect address, or other carelessness on your part.

Far and away the best way to "ship" a computer is for buyer and seller to make a face-to-face transfer. Take the computer to the buyer, plug it in, prove that it works, and walk away with a signed receipt of goods and cash or its equivalent. Or have the buyer come to your office or home, prove that the machine works, and crate it up and bid him farewell—after he signs the paper that says he's received the computer and has paid you in full. This is safe and simple.

DOING IT RIGHT

It's painful to see a computer deal fall through because the machine arrived in pieces or vanished in the mail. By following the advice in this chapter, you'll maximize your chances of actually pocketing the cash from the deal. As a general rule, follow the maxim of futurist Herman Kahn: Think the Unthinkable.

Randall's Rules

→ You might like the buyer, but that's no reason to let him or her see your financial documents and personal correspondence.

→ A clean machine is important, but a *working* clean machine is even more important.

→ A computer isn't really sold until the buyer is happy; Hell hath no fury like a buyer who gets a busted board.

CHAPTER 9

SPECIAL ISSUES FOR CORPORATE TRADERS

Selling and Buying
by the Pallet

◆►

Randall's Notebook

April 5, 1987

Boston, Massachusetts

◆►

Ah, IBM's introduction of the PS/2 line three days ago is music to our bank account. Major corporations will dump their "old" machines as predictably as rattlesnakes shed their skins. It's almost a biological urge, the way they purge the old to make way for the new. We aren't too surprised that a major utility company has already called to see if we can move two floors' worth of IBM ATs. These are executive computers, we're told, and should fetch top dollar. "We'll come right over," I say, "and tell you what they're worth."

We look at the inventory lists and agree that these are indeed "executive" machines—memory to the hilt, huge, fast, and expensive hard disks, top quality EGA monitors, 9600-baud modems—the works!

Odd, I think, as we look the hot rods over—these machines seem to be in pristine condition. Too perfect. We dig deeper and find a wealth of software packages—Lotus 1A, 2.0, and 2.01, four or five successive versions of WordStar, dBASE II, dBASE III, and dBASE III PLUS—all in their original shrink wraps. The real tip-off, though, is a case of unformatted Elephant disks—haven't been on the market for years. Clearly, these executive machines have never been used by executives or anyone else. Nevertheless, the company feels compelled to dump tens of thousands of dollars' worth of perfectly good hardware and to spend probably twice that much on a new generation of dust catchers.

And we wonder why American corporations can't compete in the global marketplace!

➤➤

CORPORATE COMPUTER POLICIES

Large corporations tend to indulge in two extreme practices as far as computer equipment is concerned. Sometimes, one company will embrace both extremes, and both extremes illustrate the point that large companies seldom base their equipment decisions on an understanding of the secondary computer market.

STATE OF THE ART AT THE TOP

The utility company anxious to unload its pristine "used" computers and replace them with the state of the art exemplifies the corporate tendency to keep top executives outfitted with the latest and the greatest. Many large corporations routinely dump all their executives' computers just to keep the state of the art on executive desks.

ASHES TO ASHES, DUST TO DUST

At the mid-management level, many corporations circulate machines from the desks of "front edge" managers and technical people down to the cubbyholes of lower-tech employees as new computer models come in. The manager's original PC goes to the secretary. In the next round, the exec gets a 386, the secretary gets the AT, and a clerk-assistant gets the original PC. Sooner or later, the original machine makes its way to the bottom rungs of the corporation. The logic carried to its conclusion dictates that the janitors of Fortune 500 companies will one day use Cray supercomputers to track the supply of toilet paper.

As computers are demoted from floor to floor, manuals, cables, monitor control knobs, and other small parts tend to disappear along with the original boxes and packaging shells. At the same time, keyboard decals, fuzzy dice, and other cosmetically degrading junk get attached to the machines. Few corporations think to maintain their machines for sale the way an individual user would, so by the time a computer has reached the bottom rung, it is usually less appealing than one sold by a private citizen.

Some corporations decide to use their computers until they're written off or they wear out. They hold on to the computers long past the time they could be sold, and the result is computer chaos—an endless churning of goods and a bottomless pit of gear gathering dust after it passes through the hands of the lowest employees on the ladder. This policy arises out of accounting principles and practices not particularly suited to a volatile technology.

Avoiding Computer Depreciation Hassles

→ Don't buy computer equipment. Rent or lease it from a lessor who provides (without penalty) for your returning leased machines for upgrading. That way, you can dump obsolete machines back on their owner.

→ Depreciate the equipment you own on a schedule that reflects the real market so that your equipment reaches zero on your books at about the same time as the value in the secondary market approaches zero. On a regular basis, reevaluate the estimated useful life of your computer equipment.

→ Use a rapid depreciation schedule, and plan to sell the equipment for more than its value on your books as soon as you have a pressing need to upgrade.

Don't let a depreciation strategy saddle your company with a pile of machines that have no market value and that keep some of your employees tied to old computer technology that's incompatible with equipment you use in other parts of the company.

A corporation's computer depreciation schedule might be based on tables for normal assets, but computer antiques that still have dollar value on the corporation's books might be worthless in the cash market.

Keeping equipment until it is fully depreciated might not be the best way to handle the "brains" of the working staff, either. An old machine can be an albatross that limits the work that the staff can do. And lower-level staff might have computers on their desks that are incompatible with the equipment used by more senior members of the corporation—all because of inappropriate depreciation accounting.

LEGITIMATE CORPORATE TECHNOLOGY CHANGE

Corporations have good reasons for mass changes in technology, too. Some corporations must sell their large lots of computers for reasons unrelated to the age of the equipment. A large lot can go up for sale because the company changes its technical direction or because a merger has taken place and the new, combined entity wants to standardize. The company might decide to change its level of technology from the IBM PC or AT bus to IBM's Micro Channel Architecture, or from IBMs to Apples, or from one network to another, or from a dedicated cluster of word processors to a network of personal computers outfitted with a company-wide word processing choice. Such decisions render a pile of computers obsolete to the company even though the equipment is fully functional and useful to a buyer with different needs or a different level of technical requirements.

THE CORPORATE SELLING PROBLEM

The need to unload almost new computers or to continually flush computers through the system creates unique selling problems for corporations and unique opportunities for buyers.

What makes corporate traders so different from everyone else? The key difference between an individual with a computer or two and a corporation with a department's worth is bulk. Big corporations don't do anything in a small way. They buy big, and they sell big. They also expect massive discounts when they buy gear, and by some perverse logic, they expect buyers to pay more for a bulk lot of computers: "Aren't buyers really paying for the opportunity to snag a perfectly matched set of computers at one shot?"

Unfortunately, the only thing most people care about buying in matched sets is luggage. The chances of someone's needing two dozen identically configured machines is rare unless the buyer happens to be another big corporation. Most Fortune 500 companies buy their computers new—it's a matter of pride.

And add-in goodies don't really enhance the value of a used computer. If a company has 20 machines with a peculiar hardware configuration, all they have to sell is 20 odd ducks. Buyers of the odd ducks believe that they're doing the corporate seller a favor and that they should be entitled to a deep discount.

SELLING IN BULK

Unloading a lot of computers is a much bigger job than selling one or two machines. The last thing a manager needs is the task of selling a few dozen computers to a few dozen buyers. Imagine the planning and energy required to sell a department's worth of computers to different individuals with unique needs.

Then there's the problem of advertising the goods. If a big corporation ran an ad in the newspaper, someone would have to answer inquiries and take small orders. Each computer would have to be boxed up and sent to a different person, and the corporation would have to assume some degree of responsibility for each buyer's satisfaction.

The job of unloading a cluster of used computers usually falls on the corporate microcomputer manager. The advice that follows should help that manager prepare for computer sales over the long range.

Maintaining and Tracking Equipment

Hold on to the boxes and packing materials for all the computers you buy. And keep all the parts for your machines intact. Don't cannibalize. Discourage employees from individualizing their computers with stickers and decals, too. Give them the tools and encouragement they need to keep their machines in standard configuration and good working order. Replace broken and lost parts with standard parts.

Maintain a database of all computer equipment your corporation has ever bought. We show suggested fields for the database records below. Lacking this information tool, the manager must rummage through remnants and shake out the storeroom. Houseclean annually, and sell or donate all computer hardware that's been replaced or displaced and is now sitting idle.

Corporate Computer Resource Database
Recommended Record Fields

DEVICE

    Type: _____ Make: _____ Model: _____

    RAM: _____ Drives: _____ Monitor: _____

    Integral peripherals: _____ Other: _____

LOCATION

    Asset #: _____ Serial #: _____

SOURCE

    Vendor: _____ Salesperson: _____

    Invoice #: _____ Price paid: _____ Date of purchase: _____

    Duty cycle: _____

VALUATION

    Residual Asset Value: _____

    Depreciation Schedule: _____

    Current replacement cost: _____

DISPOSITION

    Internal: _____ Sales: _____ Donated: _____

Getting Ready for the Sale

Whether you have a dozen PCs or a gross, be prepared to move those machines if your corporation must upgrade or liquidate its assets.

- Anticipate the disposition of your PCs, and assign staff to develop a plan for moving the equipment.

- Shop for buyers with the same care you put into shopping for sellers of new equipment. Your disposition agent and your purchasing agent can work together and often find a trade-in deal with a retail vendor that optimizes the return on your equipment investment.

Choosing a Selling Outlet

As you consider the best way to unload your company's obsolete machines, note that the lower you go in the list that follows, the lower the return.

Individual sales

Yes, we just said that this kind of sale is a pain in the neck, but if you can deal with the pain or can set up a sales facility, this option generates the most cash. Be sure that the cost of making sales justifies the return. If you can't handle individual sales, *don't* try them—you're just buying into a lot of frustration.

Auctions

If you don't have a lot of gear to move, an auction is not a viable option—most auctioneers aren't interested in a few pieces. If you are moving a lot of equipment—a whole department's worth or a whole company's worth—an auction can be a good way to clear the shelf.

Auctions often fetch top prices for equipment. At computer auctions, the public often drives the prices to near or even above current retail value. After the demise of Software Arts, founder Dan Bricklin commented that he actually sold some equipment at his auction for more than he had originally paid. How does this happen? If the auctioneer is skillful, he or she creates a frenzied atmosphere in which the buyers voraciously bid against each other without much rhyme or reason. Afterward, successful bidders probably experience the worst bellyaches of their lives as they realize that they've paid the equivalent of retail prices for equipment three years off warranty.

Trade-ins on new equipment

If you are replacing older computers with new ones, shop around for a vendor who will take the older machines on trade-in. Then negotiate for a great deal. The retail outfit makes its money on the new sale, so it can be flexible on the trade-in price. Few retailers are set up for bulk trade-ins, but the ones who are wind up with thriving businesses in new and used equipment. If your vendor doesn't take trade-ins, push the issue. Refer him or her to Appendix D of this book, "Tips for Retail Computer Stores." If the sale is large enough, the vendor can arrange for a third party to handle the used equipment (relieving you of that job) and then turn around and sell you the new equipment.

Liquidators

Don't count on liquidators to have a good idea of fair market price— they're not in the business of giving you a great deal. Most liquidators offer pennies on the dollar, preying on your need to move the computers out the door with minimum hassle. Always get several competitive bids from liquidators.

Finding Internal Selling Options

The more legwork the corporation can internalize, the greater the cash return on the computers. Selling a lot of computers one at a time might be out of the question, but other "work-intensive" methods can dispose of the equipment at an advantage to the corporation.

Sales to staff

Selling computers to corporate staff members increases the corporation's ability to have employees take work home and telecommute via modem (and might give the employees a tax break on the purchase). Such a move increases your staff's capabilities and supports the education of their children. Some companies even work out lenient payroll deduction plans that make it easier for employees to buy machines. If your company doesn't have a policy regarding PC sales to employees, it should consider creating one.

Passing computers down

Move those computers down through the ranks until the corporation is saturated. Why *shouldn't* the janitors use computers to track their supplies and manage their inventories and maintenance schedules? Maybe they don't need a Cray supercomputer, but even an entry-level PC can increase efficiency in almost any department of a company. Before a company throws out a computer or sells one for a song, it should be sure that every potential user has one on his or her desk. In a competitive world, everyone should be able to work as smart as possible.

Sales to another division

Many large corporations have divisions spread out all over the world. For such companies, we advise an internal redeployment program in which excess assets from one location are moved to another. One large corporation bought a Boston Computer Exchange manual, the same one we sell to new exchange "Seats," so that it could efficiently reallocate its internal resources. This company is so large and geographically spread out that it actually operates as a self-contained, minisecondary market, maintaining an active database of all machines in circulation, with "buyers" and "sellers" and lots of "on the books" transactions.

The idea of divisions treating each other as customers is nothing new in corporate accounting, especially in the manufacturing sector. But the idea of redeploying equipment by creating an internal secondary market is a novel twist that any large company with a substantial investment in PC assets should consider. Internal "sales" can save time and energy and ensure that usable technology is recycled into the right hands at the right time.

CORPORATE BUYING

At the time of this writing, few companies buy computers in bulk on the used market. The ones that do tend not to be the Fortune 500 variety. The next tier of large corporations, the ones that watch their money closely, are always looking for ways to cut costs. These companies are willing to investigate the potential savings of buying computers with a past.

BUYING IN BULK

Companies that realize the wisdom of buying in bulk in the secondary market enjoy substantial savings on their equipment, and they can often outfit an entire department with a desirable level of technology in one fell swoop. One appropriate buyer for bulk lots of used equipment is the company that has decided to keep its not-fully depreciated older computers and add units to its installed base. Typically, this will be a company with a large investment in PC-era or AT-era computers that wants to preserve its investment. Rather than buy new computers with configurations different from the old, it buys another company's used equipment in bulk and maintains compatibility. Subject to certain limitations, the Internal Revenue Code allows individuals and corporations to expense the cost of up to $10,000 of used as well as new computer equipment as opposed to capitalizing and depreciating the gear over five years.

Some large corporations have saved hundreds of thousands of dollars buying large lots of computers in the used equipment market. None would want its name to appear in this context, but savvy corporate buyers are often on the lookout for great buys. One procurement manager had an employment contract in which he got to keep a percentage of the savings he gleaned for the corporation. His technical staff had decided to focus on the IBM AT rather than move on to the new PS/2 line. Instead of buying questionable new AT clones, this

Bulk Buying Strategies

↦ Buy for eventual resale. Whatever you buy, you will eventually resell, so go for value, quality, and standard equipment. Clones don't hold their value in bulk any more than they do individually.

↦ Go for the discount. If you are buying in bulk, you are entitled to a bulk discount. Remember, you're helping someone with a bulk problem, so expect to be rewarded for your buying volume. Never succumb to the logic that the seller is doing you a favor by making a truckload of identical machines available to you in one lot.

↦ Buy a little more than you need. It's better to have a few extra used machines than too few. You'll want them for parts, for spares, and for future growth.

↦ Don't break up a lot. It's better to buy what the seller has in a lot than to break up the lot (unless, of course, the seller's lot is 10 times what you can use). In general, you can get a better price on the seller's lot than on a lot size you insist on.

↦ Pay for the configuration you want. If your configuration of choice calls for monochrome monitors and the volume lot has VGA cards and color monitors, offer what you'd pay for mono-equipped machines. You might get the color monitors for "free."

procurement officer bought IBM ATs as they came off other corporations' leases. The company saved bundles and continued to use genuine IBM products. And the procurement officer pocketed enough money to buy a BMW—used.

Some companies maintain a large number of older PCs that they cannibalize as they need parts for their active machines. Others specifically need a batch of disk drives, display adapters, or some other component to maintain their current PC fleet. For these companies, it sometimes pays to make a bulk purchase of PCs from another company, transplant the needed parts, and then sell the remains of the older PCs as best they can or hold the parts in inventory. This often turns out to be the cheapest way to keep a department's worth of PCs operational. The company micro manager's job description might include maintaining a supply of machines in storage and getting another system up and running at any time in just a few hours. Cannibalizing can be the most expedient way to do the job.

Choosing the Best Sources for Bulk Buying

The following sources are listed in order of desirability—the higher the source on this list, the better the price and the more current the machines you're likely to find. Of course, each situation presents unique opportunities and pitfalls, but the following list can serve as a starting point for your pricing investigations.

Corporations

If you have time, energy, and a regular need for more computers, it pays to find the assets recovery staff at one or more local corporations. Let them know what you want, and find out whether you can buy directly as they displace their old computers. Situations such as this are rare, and the fit can be odd. But if you do make a connection, you'll find yourself with a terrific deal because you won't buy through intermediaries or incur extra expenses.

Bankruptcy proceedings

Unless it pertains to his own company, Chapter 11 is music to the ears of a computer liquidator or broker. When a company goes bust, there are always PCs to be sold. The person who can appear on the doorstep with a truck and a check can often get a fantastic bargain. The trustees will have to handle a lot of legal details and paperwork, but the prices are great.

The downside to buying computers through a bankruptcy calls for your attention to some unpleasant circumstances. Newly unemployed staff of a company in the throes of bankruptcy sometimes appropriate PCs to vent their anger on the company that has folded up around them. In numerous cases in which the Exchange has been called in to handle the disposition of a bankrupt company's PC assets, we've found that the actual number of computers on the premises is fewer than the number on the manager's asset list.

If computers aren't stolen outright by disgruntled staff, we frequently find missing or vandalized pieces. In one instance, we found large lag bolts driven through the S keys of all the keyboards. Someone sent the message, "We got screwed."

If you buy in bulk from a bankrupt company, count those computers and then check them out thoroughly.

Leasing companies

Leasing companies are a great untapped resource for bulk equipment buying. They're constantly trying to get rid of the computers they've sent out on lease and received back, and from time to time they have a good stock of used equipment for sale. Leasing companies want to move returned machines as quickly as possible for a small profit because they've already made their money in the lease arrangement.

Auctions

As noted in this chapter under "Choosing the Best Selling Outlet," auctions often turn into opportunities to pay top dollar for out-of-date equipment. Have a definite limit in mind, and quash any impulse to "play"—if you get carried away, you're finished. To protect yourself, know the going prices. (We usually take the *BoCoEx Index* with us to auctions. As soon as the bidding for a particular configuration exceeds the index level, we drop out.)

And go to the auction with a specific list of equipment on which you will bid. Don't be tempted by something that's "just too good a bargain to pass up." At every auction someone goes home with the equivalent of an imitation-silk, pink-striped lampshade.

Liquidators

The key in dealing with liquidators is to negotiate. Know your prices. Remember that the liquidator bought cheap from a desperate seller and paid pennies on the dollar. Offer a few more pennies and stand firm. The liquidator has no interest in keeping the equipment any longer than necessary—the name of the liquidator's game is a quick sale at a reasonable profit.

Public agencies

Government agencies and other public organizations, such as universities, often sell lots of used equipment to bidders. If you need a pile of gear and don't mind filling out odd requests for bids, get on the bid list by contacting various public agencies and informing them that you're in the market for bulk computer equipment. Buying through government bidding is cumbersome and slow. And government agencies and universities usually hang on to equipment until it's truly archaic. (Have you ever sat behind a government-issue army surplus desk?) The government takes its time handling bids, too, so equipment can actually be too old for your needs by the time it gets into your hands. Bidding is for odd lots, and the bid lots are often broken-up systems. You might get a great deal, but it might be of little value without the other pieces, which might have been sold as part of another lot. Know exactly what you are looking for and what you're bidding on before you open your mouth.

Computers sit in corporate offices all over the world. Some are underused, and others can't keep up with the work demand. Often, older computers hold employees back from achieving greater productivity. Every company owes its employees the tools they need. A corporation should keep upgrading its PC stock by pushing older computers down the line and eventually out the door—to someone else ready to move up to a "new" technology.

Randall's Rules

↦ Don't let an accountant's depreciation strategy govern the level of technology at which your company works.

↦ If you buy well and sell well, you can probably keep your job.

↦ Look under your nose before you sell—the best place for your old computers might be the desks down the hall.

CHAPTER 10

THE LAST RUNG

Donating vs. Selling Your Computer

◆▸

Randall's Notebook
December 24, 1987
Boston, Massachusetts

◆▸

This is the saddest day before Christmas I've ever been through. At four
o'clock, Cam and I are packing up to head home when a call comes in
from Father Malcolm McDuff. Can I help him with a computer prob-
lem at his refugee training center? I don't usually make house calls, es-
pecially hours before Christmas Eve, but how can I turn down someone
with a name like "Father McDuff"? Besides, the training center is only
a few blocks away.

I walk to the center, where I'm greeted by a cheery man in his
sixties, with a full head of snow white hair. "Ah, good of you to brave
the weather to come see us," he says with a twinkle in his eye.

He explains that six months ago he received a donated IBM
DisplayWriter. He'd hoped to use it to train refugees as word processors
so that they could earn enough money to support themselves. But the
ancient DisplayWriter (featuring 8-inch floppy disk drives and a
chassis big enough to sleep six) hadn't worked. Or Father McDuff and
the volunteers hadn't known how to make it work. Father McDuff
put out a call for more equipment, and well-meaning donors have

responded with more castaways. In three months the padre has assembled quite a computer museum. His inventory includes, among other gems:

1 TI-99 4/A.

1 Epson HX-20 with tape cassette.

1 Radio Shack Model 100.

1 Columbia Portable computer.

3 Commodore 64s with no disk drives.

4 Apple II +s, one without a case.

1 Osborne I with a 5-inch screen.

1 Wang 2200.

1 broken 16KB IBM PC with one drive and no monitor.

4 hybrid clones, made of parts from manufacturers I've never heard of. One clone has a gaping hole where the disk drives should be, and one doesn't have a power supply.

In the midst of this high-tech circus sits a table stacked high with parts—modems, asynch cards, memory cards, printer heads, tractor feed gears, disk drives, and so on. Wires, plugs, and chips are strewn from one end of the table to the other. I imagine that this is what an IBM service center would look like after a nuclear war.

Even if the volunteers knew how to manage all the hardware in the center, they certainly wouldn't have the time to learn and teach all the individual software programs for each machine. It's hopeless.

"Well, Lad, how can we get all this fine equipment working?" Father McDuff asks. "We have to help these people get jobs and feed their families."

Thirty pairs of eyes stare at me as I muster, "Let us pray."

◆▶

ISLANDS OF NEED

The situation at Father McDuff's training center would have been amusing, but a roomful of people sat waiting for me to "fix" their meal tickets. Of course, there was nothing I could do. I couldn't even operate most of the computers, let alone train people on them. Even if I could, what good would it do? The donors were well intentioned, but the chances of any of the refugees' learning marketable skills from the center's hodgepodge of machines were depressingly slim. Knowing how to use the text editor of a Radio Shack Model 100 won't get you into the executive suite of a company today. A homogeneous group of any of the computers that would run even old versions of today's software would have been a lot closer to a training center than the odd assortment of mismatched equipment.

Contrast the situation in a neighboring state at a rehabilitation center for the blind. This organization had carefully engineered a donation plan, designating itself a receiving point for the original Compaq Portable computer, an early DOS machine with floppy disk drives. They specialized. At the risk of seeming haughty by turning down donations, they'd rejected offers that didn't match their development strategy and redirected machines that didn't "fit" to other organizations that could use them.

A foundation had publicized their need for the old Compaqs, so the center found itself with a healthy supply of the machines they wanted. One outplacement manager in the asset recovery department of a local corporation heard about the center's needs and arranged for a company truck to deliver 22 Portables to the organization's front door.

What about software? Within a week after the center notified a large Compaq users group about the donation program, the members rallied to the cause and contributed hundreds of useful software programs, some current, some public domain, and some "classic." The center was well equipped for all kinds of computing—word processing, database management, spreadsheets, and so on. And the center had received enough copies of some software to be able to focus its attention on the most widely installed programs.

As the computers rolled in the door, the center's volunteers became proficient at scavenging parts from "surplus" machines. Those parts for repair ensured a core of computers in tip-top shape, always ready.

You might wonder how a center for the blind would use computers. As the final step in the plan, the center enlisted the help of a local engineering professor to design a simple board that allowed the Compaqs to function as speech synthesizers. Now the center's blind can earn a living on their computers through word processing, data entry, mailing list maintenance, and other clerical tasks.

Both Father McDuff's refugee training center and the rehabilitation center for the blind declared themselves "islands of need," hoping to receive help from the "thousand points of light" potentially illuminating our nation. In the case of the refugee center, the call was, in effect, blind—"We'll take anything you don't want!" The rehabilitation center for the blind was more clear sighted. The center launched a well-thought-out campaign to secure reliable machines that would run current generation software yet would be too slow for most corporate users. This boosted their chances that corporations would readily supply the models the center wanted. Whereas the refugee training center struggled with an impossible mix of hardware, operating systems, and software, the center for the blind recognized the importance of asking for one brand, one model. As a result, the center for the blind became expert in the management and use of one generation of Compaq technology, ensuring that it would always have a plentiful supply of working machines and software on hand.

When donations are properly handled, everyone wins. The people who need computers the most and can afford them the least get their gear, and the businesses that donate the computers get goodwill, tax benefits, and the opportunity to move on to the next level of computer performance.

In donations to job and rehabilitation centers, everyone can win further. The donor organization has access to the best center trainees, and the best trainees have an inside track into good jobs. If the island of need is close to the equipment donor, the donor can enhance the value of the gift by providing on-site training and receive even more tax benefits.

Such arrangements can be ideal, but computer donations can also turn into a nightmare for both parties. In this chapter, we'll look at the donation issue from both sides of the fence, showing you how to create symbiotic relationships in which both parties benefit.

THE GIVING SIDE

There's no point in donating something just to move it out of the stockroom. That can solve your problem, but it doesn't necessarily help the receiving party, and it can nullify further use of the computer. If you don't place your computer with an organization that knows what to do with it and how to maintain it, you're simply adding to their frustration. The critical concept is *fit*. A bad fit is a drain on the recipient's already strained resources because the organization will either hire someone to try to "straighten it all out" or pay someone to haul the equipment away.

DONATION CHANNELS

How do you find out what kinds of equipment various organizations need? You have two choices: Open up the phone book and start calling The United Way, churches, temples, or the local Boy Scout troops; or contact experts and organizations that specialize in donations and maintain lists of qualified donees. The first approach is time-consuming, and you'll be likely to leave your computer(s) in the wrong place. The second approach saves you time and headaches and ensures that your equipment reaches a new home where it fits. Here are some sources of information about how to put your outmoded computers where they'll do the most good.

Clearinghouses

Several national clearinghouses maintain lists of organizations that want specific brands and models of computers and peripherals. Some match computers from large organizations with groups in need. (See Appendix B.) Some clearinghouses are devoted to the handicapped, some deal with job training, and others focus on groups that coordinate relief efforts outside the US.

The National Cristina Foundation (Pelham Manor, New York), for example, places computers with rehabilitation centers for the handicapped. The Foundation serves a large number of organizations and can place almost any type of computer with a recipient who needs it. Special provisions of the Internal Revenue Code allow more generous deductions for certain donations to organizations who care for the ill, the needy, or infants. (See "Special Donation Situations," later in this chapter.")

Usually, clearinghouses don't charge fees to donors. Recipients are always on tight budgets, though, so your covering costs of shipping is a boost to them. If you do get a line on an organization, don't simply ship your computer to the organization or the clearinghouse! Find out what equipment the organization wants, and send your computers to the location it specifies.

Brokers

Local and national computer brokers are besieged with calls from organizations looking for donations. Many brokers keep a list of these groups and charge a modest processing fee to handle the matchmaking. The Boston Computer Exchange, for instance, maintains a list of organizations that want donations. Unfortunately, the potential recipients outnumber donors by about 50 to 1. The organizations range from community playhouses and veterans' hospitals to the YMCA/ YWCA, refugee centers, and groups that supply food to starving Ethiopians.

Used Computer Stores

Organizations seeking computers will often check with used computer stores for exceptional deals. Some stores eagerly pass on the information to interested donors.

Retail Computer Stores

Some retail shops maintain a list of local recipients. As a way to encourage the disposition of hardware, retail vendors encourage and facilitate the donation or generous sale of machines—the goodwill boosts their sales. (See Appendix D.) Some retail computer operations will actually tell you, "Oh, the Good Samaritans always buy Apple IIs and Imagewriter printers," or "The Home for Orphaned Children is strictly an IBM shop."

In addition to seeking "pure" donations, some recipient organizations have modest budgets or get money through fundraisers and gifts for buying equipment outright. If you have a computer you are willing to sell for the cost of shipping, plenty of organizations can come up with a small sum of money for it. Retail outlets can be a good way to get a handle on potential recipients. (For tax purposes, such a transaction would be considered part sale and part gift. Your tax advisor should be able to help you apply the relevant IRS rulings.)

Whether you use a clearinghouse or find a recipient organization through a store or your own efforts, be ready to furnish a lot of information about the equipment. If you have the information in front of you when you're ready to offer the gear, you'll save everyone time and energy. The worksheets shown on the next three pages will help you arrange the best match.

Randall's Computer Donor Worksheet

COMPUTER

Date purchased: _____ Original cost: _____

Ordinary income property? (Y/N): _____

Tax depreciation up to the date of donation: _____

Make: _____ Model: _____

Processor: _____ Operating system: _____

Disk drives

Floppy 1   Size: _____   Format: _____

Floppy 2   Size: _____   Format: _____

Hard disk 1   Size: _____   Internal _____   External _____

Hard disk 2   Size: _____   Internal _____   External _____

Other: _____

I/O ports: Serial (#) _____   Parallel (#) _____

Display

Graphics card type: _____

Monitor manufacturer: _____

Monitor type: Monochrome _____   Color _____

Other add-on or add-in cards: _____

_____

_____

Software included with equipment: _____

_____

Current market price (get it appraised) for tax purposes: _____

CONDITION OF THE EQUIPMENT

Occasionally, an organization will accept broken equipment for use in their spare parts bank. A group like the rehabilitation center for the blind mentioned earlier, for example, will take any Compaq Portable, in any state, because they know they can always salvage something, even if only a control knob for the monitor or a slot cover.

In general, though, defunct gear is of no value to charitable or not-for-profit organizations, especially those with little technical

Randall's Peripherals Donor Worksheet

Printer

    Date purchased: _____ Original cost: _____

    Make: _____ Model: _____

    Accessories: _____

Modem

    Date purchased: _____ Original cost: _____

    Make: _____ Model: _____

    Baud rate: _____

Pointing devices

    Mouse

        Date purchased: _____ Original cost: _____

        Make: _____ Model: _____

    Track ball

        Date purchased: _____ Original cost: _____

        Make: _____ Model: _____

    Digitizing pen

        Date purchased: _____ Original cost: _____

        Make: _____ Model: _____

Tape drives

    Date purchased: _____ Original cost: _____

    Make: _____ Model: _____

    Tape format: _____

Miscellaneous

    Surge suppressors, etc.: _____

expertise. The most pathetic calls we get at the Exchange are from people who have a pressing need, who have received computer equipment, but who can't get the equipment to do anything at all. The cost of repair is prohibitive to such organizations, and few repair services donate time, so the equipment is transformed from a hopeful ray of light into an expense or into scrap for the dumpster. A working old dinosaur is more valuable to recipients than a broken state-of-the-art system.

Randall's Donee Organization Worksheet

501(c)(3) organization? (Y/N): _____

  Current equipment: _____

_____

_____

  Equipment needs: _____

_____

_____

  Current software: _____

_____

_____

  Level of service or maintenance recipient can provide:

_____

_____

DONATING SOFTWARE

It seems logical to pass along outdated programs, but most software licenses forbid the transfer of programs, even outdated releases, without explicit permission from the publisher. (See "Legal Issues" in Chapter 7.) In 1990, WordPerfect Corporation broke ground when it allowed users of version 5.1 of its word processing program to donate prior versions to elementary and secondary schools. Hundreds of corporations seized the opportunity to donate their older software. Check with your software publisher before passing along your programs, no matter how good your intentions.

TAX BENEFITS

If you make a donation to a "qualified tax exempt organization" (as defined in section 170(c) of the Internal Revenue Code), the donation might be tax deductible. In general, you can deduct the fair market value of the computer, defined in Regulation 1.170A-1(c) of the Code as "the price at which the computer would change hands between a willing buyer and a willing seller, neither being under any compulsion to buy or sell, and both having reasonable knowledge of relevant facts."

Establishing fair market value is the key issue. At the Boston Computer Exchange, we calculate the system's worth as though the seller were willing to wait for a buyer. Even derelict equipment still has some cash value. We might have only one buyer per year for the original CP/M Kaypro 2, but it still has value. We might have listings for 100 Kaypro 2s in the same year. One sale sets a value for the rest of the machines. The owner of the 101st Kaypro 2 could donate the machine and for tax purposes use the sale price of the last Kaypro 2 transaction as the fair market value of the computer.

When there is a more active cash market for a computer make and model, the most current cash price offered for the computer should set its donation value. For computers for which there are no buyers and no cash market, the value would be its price at its last trade depreciated on a normal depreciation curve.

Special Donation Situations

In some cases, unique Internal Revenue Code rules apply in determining the amount that can be deducted for a contribution. According to CPA Alan Muster of the Newton, Massachusetts, firm Muster & Berardi, a leading authority on computer donation tax issues, you must note numerous important Internal Revenue Code provisions when you donate a computer. As an example of the complexity of the laws, Muster explains two that commonly affect corporations that donate computer equipment:

1. If the company making the donation has already depreciated the computers, the deduction is limited to the lesser of the fair market value or the remaining basis in the equipment.

    For example, if a company purchased $100,000 worth of computers in 1986, the accumulated depreciation taken on tax returns through 1989 would be $79,000. Let's assume that the company wants to donate the entire lot of computers. Even though the fair market value for the lot is $25,000, the maximum donation value for income tax deduction purposes would be $21,000 (the remaining basis).

If the computers were fully depreciated, the company's adjusted basis in the equipment would be $0, and therefore the deduction would be $0. In that case, it might be more prudent to sell the equipment and donate the cash to an organization. Cash donations are usually deductible in full, provided that certain other tax-sensitive criteria are met.

This rule applies regardless of the exempt status of the recipient. The rule also assumes that the equipment has not appreciated in value since its acquisition.

2. If the computer(s) to be given away represents "ordinary income property" for the donor (the inventory of a computer manufacturer or computer retailer, for example), the fair market value of the equipment must be reduced by the amount of gain that a sale in the regular course of business would produce.

For example, if a computer maker wants to donate computers that have a fair market value of $60,000 and an inventoried value of $40,000, the allowable deduction would be $40,000 ($60,000 – [60,000–40,000]).

A special provision of this rule applies if the company donates computer inventory and certain other property to 501(c)(3) organizations that will use the equipment solely for care of the ill, the needy, or infants. According to this special provision, the deduction of the company in the example above would increase to $42,000.

As you can see from just these two examples, the tax laws that pertain to computer donations are complex. If you contemplate a donation primarily for tax purposes, consult your tax advisor so that your company will get the maximum deductions allowed by the Internal Revenue Code.

ADDITIONAL BENEFITS OF DONATING EQUIPMENT

The cost of making a donation might be zero or negligible. If the recipients are local, they can usually find a truck to haul equipment away. But a charitable donor who can include the cost of shipping or transport as part of the donation can really help the recipients. For some computers, the cost of shipping exceeds the value of the equipment to anyone. We know of one corporate storeroom full of derelict mainframe computer equipment that has less value than the cost of moving it to a new location. It rusts where it sits.

WHEN TO SELL AND WHEN TO DONATE

Deciding to donate rather than to sell a computer is a decision you probably won't base simply on economics. You need to evaluate the nonfinancial benefits you'll receive from making a donation.

From a fiscal perspective, a computer whose value has been depreciated to a low level costs more to sell than the cash you'd lose by donating it. Searching for a buyer and handling the sale can be time-consuming and expensive, so getting that very last dollar might cost more than a dollar. The cost of a donation is very low. The time involved is less than the time needed to make a sale, especially if you have a hard-to-move machine.

ADOPTING AN ORGANIZATION

The ideal strategy for making donations is for the donor to adopt an organization. Select an organization and set up an ongoing conduit to them. In addition to excess computers, you can provide them with office gear, supplies, and other goods. Adoption of an organization gives you a consistent recipient of your excess equipment and a standing tax deduction arrangement. The recipient knows that there will be a more or less consistent supply of gear and perhaps some additional benefits in the form of volunteer time from the donor's staff.

First, find an organization or two that you really like, whose work is aligned with the hearts and minds of you and your organization. The optimal fit occurs when the work of a corporation is in harmony with the work of a not-for-profit organization. An electricity utility adopts an organization that teaches the public about energy awareness, for example. Or a sporting goods company adopts a junior baseball league. Or a service company with a constant need for entry-level staff donates equipment to a training center. Or an eyeglass maker adopts a center for vision research. Find a recipient whose work is in an area that appeals to you, whose politics agree with yours, or whose work parallels your own or supports your own.

Whatever the reason, adopt a favored group and start to do steady "business" with it. This not only simplifies your problem of moving older equipment out the door, but if you involve your staff, encouraging them to devote off-hours time to training, support, and maintenance, you'll also show the community at large that your company really cares about *all* its "stakeholders," whether they're paddling in the mainstream or struggling in the backwaters.

THE RECEIVING SIDE

If you're an organization that wants to receive free gear, you have two information-related obligations. First, as we showed earlier, you must choose a model or promulgate a standard for internal use. Then you have to get the word out. Let's take a look at both activities.

IDENTIFYING YOUR NEEDS

In order to select a computer standard for your organization, you must know what your people will be doing with the computers.

Training People to Near-Business Standards

If you're training people to work in the real world, they'll need to demonstrate proficiency with common business tools. Training is about using the tools, whether they are IBM PCs, Macintoshes, or Wang word processors. The important thing is to use something close to a standard business tool even if it isn't exactly the configuration the trainee will use in the work force. Computers used in a real office have hard disks, but training with floppy disk drive models is a closer approximation than training with chalk and pencils.

As for software, training with programs such as Word, WordPerfect, Lotus 1-2-3, and dBASE would be ideal. The closer you can come to the current standards, the better off your graduates will be when they hit the streets. But be realistic. You won't receive copies of the current releases of major software programs. Earlier generations of mainstream software are often available from donors and are still excellent introductory training tools. The fundamentals of spreadsheets, for example, haven't really changed since the days of VisiCalc.

Identify the optimum job a training center graduate can aspire to, and then identify the computers that do the job. Trace that model back a generation or two, and see if early models are available for donation. Set your standard make, model, and software, and get the word out.

Performing Internal Administrative Tasks

Most not-for-profits need word processing capabilities for letters and reports. Early PCs, even the older CP/M machines and the original IBM PCs or the first Macintosh computers, will do it. After all, that is exactly what the leading edge computers of the early 1980s were doing. Word processing on the most primitive dedicated word processor is such a step ahead of typewriters that any not-for-profit will make great gains with even an ancient tool.

Every not-for-profit we encounter wants a full state-of-the-art desktop publishing system, but it really could get a great deal done with the simplest word processing system. A dual floppy disk machine with a monochrome monitor and a 10 characters per second printer are a big advance for a paper-and-pencil outfit. Not-for-profit organizations can climb the same computer ladder corporate America has, a rung or two further down.

Keeping the Books

Every not-for-profit organization needs to keep financial records if it is to comply with IRS rules. And even if the organization deals with only small sums, it needs to track its dollars carefully. An Osborne I, an Apple II, a Commodore, or a single floppy disk drive IBM PC provides starting power for making the transition from a paper bookkeeping system to an electronic system.

Professional fundraising software can perform exotic number crunching and reporting tricks, but even first generation spreadsheets such as VisiCalc and Multiplan can do wonders for organizations used to working with hand-held calculators. Almost all first generation personal computers can run some kind of spreadsheet or accounting program. Set a minimum standard, and don't be turned off by the comparatively low performance of an older machine. Any step toward electronic bookkeeping is a step in the right direction.

Maintaining Donation Histories and Mailing Lists

Most not-for-profits are in the donation seeking business, which means they must maintain mailing lists, generate mail merge letters, and do other direct mail activities. Sending mailings calls for a database program and a system that can handle the mailing list size the organization manages.

Most database programs are hideously slow on floppy disk systems because database programs tend to be "I/O intensive," meaning that they constantly read from and write to the disk containing data.

And floppies fill up pretty quickly, so for large databases, you need hard disk storage. Hard disks might be essential to your organization's computing scheme.

CREATING A STANDARD

Once you have identified your needs and decided what kind of computers your organization needs, the next step is to develop a standards plan. Here are some guidelines:

- Specialize in one manufacturer and preferably one model or family of models, and stick with this solid foundation you can build on later.

- Don't waste your time looking for donations of a peculiar off-brand; you might spend the rest of your life waiting for the phone to ring.

- Try to find models just out of vogue. At the time of this writing, for instance, many companies are trying to sell or give away IBM XTs with 10-megabyte hard disks. The machines generally aren't worth enough to a corporation or small business to upgrade with high capacity disks. The market has a rich supply of these machines right now. Corporations and individuals aren't throwing the machines away, but almost any present owner of an IBM XT era computer or an early Macintosh computer is looking for the next generation of computer power.

  How do you find machines that are just out of vogue? Try a computer retailer, software retailer, or broker who will divulge which companies or organizations bought a lot of a particular type of machine three years ago. If you make it clear that your purpose is to find castaway computers rather than to steal their customers, you might find a receptive ear.

■ Look for "modal" machines, machines that meet the needs of most of the general computing population. Such machines will have enough power to do most fundamental computer tasks but won't set records for speed or storage. Even so, a modal machine is likely to fill the basic needs of your organization.

GETTING THE WORD OUT

Getting a donation is about disbursing the message to everyone who should hear it. If you can reach 100 points of light with one phone call, you need to make only nine more calls to reach the other 900 points! Here's what you should do:

■ Call the clearinghouses listed in Appendix B.

■ Call local brokers and used computer stores and tell them what you're looking for. If they show any interest or offer any hope, send them a letter stating your needs. Send them reminder letters two or three times a year. Be sure they know what you want and what you'd settle for. If you're a multimachine operation, compatibility is an issue and you need to forestall potential conflicts.

   If you're a one-computer operation, virtually any machine will help. If the stores don't have ready access to donors, many at least have low-end equipment for the low budget, not-for-profit organization. For a recipient seeking a donation, this is a valuable alternative. If there are no donations available, an inexpensive PC is better than no PC.

■ Contact computer clubs and user groups and ask them to place your listing in club publications and on their electronic bulletin boards.

■ Call local volume users—banks, large corporations, institutions—to determine what and when they outplace.

- Contact retail stores to find out about recent big sales. Big buyers who acquire new equipment can have outplacement problems. Register your interests with all local retailers. A retail store will often help a client donate existing equipment because the donation paves the way for new sales.

NOT-FOR-PROFIT WHEELING AND DEALING

Even though you might receive yesterday's technology, you can still play in the major leagues of computing by retrading in the secondary market. No group illustrates this better than The Sisters of Mount Saint Mary's Abbey (fondly known at the Boston Computer Exchange as the "Sisters of the Cross and Disk Drive"). This Trappistine group makes chocolate candy and discovered that it needs a fairly powerful computer system to track orders and UPS manifests and to schedule deliveries. The sisters collected a batch of orphaned IBM System 23s and sold the old machines to a scrap dealer. The proceeds of the sale plus some candy sales cash was sufficient to buy the sisters a then state-of-the-art Compaq 386 with a substantial hard disk drive. The candy's great, and the sisters are using hardware that will meet their needs for years to come.

ACTING LOCALLY

In this era of "Think globally—Act locally," we'd like to propose that you focus on the second half and support computing efforts in your neighborhood and surrounding community. Not only does this simplify shipping, delivery, training, and support, but it allows you to see the benefits of your donation. A well-placed extra computer in your community will help to solve community problems. Unless you have a burning personal desire to support an international cause, there's no reason to put the power of your extra computer at the service of problems halfway around the world—there are plenty of problems to be solved locally. We urge you to look out your window and imagine how your computer can change the world, bit by bit.

Randall's Rules

→ No fit, no value.

→ Before you scrap any thought tool, be sure there is no one left on the planet who can use it.

→ Don't accept gear just because it's offered—there are plenty of big friends with deep pockets to choose from.

REACH FOR THE STARS

Computers began as vast projects that required the greatest minds of the era, huge financial resources, and cavernous housing. Computers were tools of the elite that helped the richest corporations and largest government agencies manage themselves while the rest of us plodded along with paper and pencils.

Today, computer power has been somewhat democratized. Millions of people around the world have computers on their desks. But billions still work with pencil and paper. The work that remains is to get computers into the hands of everyone who can put them to good use.

Personal computers are one of the bright hopes for the human species. If we deploy computer hardware intelligently, we can solve some of the intractable problems facing humanity on this planet. Let's not blow the opportunity! Here are some parting Randall's Rules for a smarter, more productive twenty-first century.

Randall's Rules

- ➥ Give people printouts and they'll file reports; give them PCs and they'll interpret the world.
- ➥ We're all on the same ladder. When you outgrow a technology, pass it down. When you acquire a technology, think of its eventual disposition.
- ➥ Your computer is one share of the collective mind—use it wisely.

APPENDIX A

TIPS FOR THE FIRST-TIME BUYER

If you've never owned a computer before, take a number of steps to make your first buying experience a pleasant and fruitful one.

First, get your vocabulary straight. If you don't know the difference between random access memory (RAM) and permanent storage, you won't be able to communicate with sophisticated sellers. Pick up a good computer glossary or dictionary.

Next, read up on the basic workings of computers. Any number of general computing books can teach you how computers work. Or you might take a course at a local junior college, community college, or high school. If you do, avoid the courses that teach programming. Millions of people use computers every day, but most couldn't write a line of programming code if their lives depended on it. And that's fine—application software (word processors, spreadsheets, databases, and so on) does all the work for you. Take a course that teaches you how to use a standard operating system and that introduces you to some common applications. You don't need to be able to design a computer or a program from scratch, but to trade in the secondary market, you need to know the role of each component in a computer system and a little about the software you'll use.

Once you're up to speed on the basics of computing, browse through books on the specific applications you're thinking of using. You'll get a good notion of the kind of hardware you ought to buy to accomplish your goals.

After you've covered the bookstore, walk over to the corner newsstand or library and pick up several current magazines devoted to the type of computer you plan to buy. For the IBM family, read *PC Magazine*, *PC World*, *PC Week*, *PC Computing*, and *PC Resource*. For the Apple family, read *MacWorld*, *MacWEEK*, *MacUser*, and *InCider*. For general information, read *InfoWorld* and *BYTE*. If you plan to use your machine for a special purpose, read the literature and newsletters devoted to your application—*Publish!* for desktop publishing, for example. The magazines do an excellent job of keeping you abreast of developments that might affect your purchase plans.

As a newcomer, you need people who can help you with your computer system and the software you intend to buy. If you buy from a used computer store, the salespeople or technical support staff can usually help you out. A private individual probably won't want to be your mentor. In that case, you should contact local computer groups, instructors at community colleges, YMCAs, high schools, and friends who have similar machines.

The issue of technical support is closely related to the issue of compatibility. If you can't readily find support for a particular computer, think about buying a machine more widely in use or one close to the current most popular machine. Compatibility really has to do with safety in numbers. It means fitting into a community of users who share tips, critique enhancement products and software, experiment with new techniques, and teach each other how to get started and get the most out of their machines. If there's more than one kind of computer in your various environments, you'll need to decide whether you want a machine compatible with the computers at work, with the computers your kids use at school, or with the computers some other community group or organization uses.

The time to be a loner is not when you buy a computer. If you're a nonconformist by nature, put your ego aside. Join the masses, and you'll never find yourself alone in a technical maze.

Finally, when you choose a machine, don't limit your sights to today. If we had a nickel for every time we've heard someone utter that famous phrase, "Oh, I'll never need more than 40 megabytes of memory," we'd be rich. Computers open doors to chambers within your mind that you never knew existed. If you have 5 uses for the computer today, you'll have 10 in two months and 20 in six months. The more you work on a computer, the more ways you'll find for the computer to reduce your drudgery and help you to work more efficiently, productively, and creatively. When you buy a computer, you begin a journey. Why limit yourself to a carriage that can make only the first leg? Think of the long haul, and buy more capacity than you think you'll need. That will get you to the next frontier. Who knows what will be available then?

RESOURCES

You'll find the resources in this list helpful as you consider selling, donating, or buying a used computer.

BLUE BOOKS

The Orion Computer Blue Book
Orion Research Corporation
1315 Main Avenue, Suite 230
Durango, CO 81301
303-247-8855

The Orion Computer Blue Book contains 21,000 individual items, including used PCs, mainframes, modems, printers, floppy and hard drives, monitors, and so on. $124.50

Computer Blue Book
National Association of Computer Dealers
13103 FM 1960 West, Suite 206
Houston, TX 77065
800-223-5264

NACD publishes the *Computer Blue Book*, a pricing guide for 18,000 items. The book includes national and international directories of manufacturers, distributors, and service companies. The *Computer Blue Book* contains a national listing of rental companies and used computer dealers, too. $15.95

DEALER ASSOCIATIONS

The following dealer associations don't publish blue books but can help you find a local dealer.

ABCD
The Microcomputer Industry Association
1515 East Woodfield Road
Schaumburg, IL 60173
708-240-1818

National Office Products Association
Computer Dealers Forum
301 North Fairfax Street
Alexandria, VA 22314
703-549-9040

COMPUTER THEFT HOTLINE

Computer Theft Hotline
National Association of Computer Dealers
800-223-5264

The hotline is a service of the National Association of Computer Dealers. A voice messaging service lets you record the serial numbers of your equipment (including CPU number, monitor number, printer number, and so on) with your name. The only way you can change the registration of ownership is to notify NACD by letter. If you are buying used equipment, verify ownership by checking with the Computer Theft Hotline. If the equipment has been stolen, you will be directed to the right person to contact at NACD.

DONATION CLEARINGHOUSES

National Cristina Foundation
42 Hillcrest Drive
Pelham Manor, NY 10803
800-CRISTINA
914-738-7494

The National Cristina Foundation is a not-for-profit organization that collects used computers of all kinds and distributes them to hundreds of organizations serving the disabled and the disadvantaged (educational institutions, rehabilitation centers, students at risk of school failure, and so on). By virtue of its large size and its network applications database and by working closely in the field with organizations to match donated equipment to the needs of groups, the Cristina Foundation ensures the maximum utility of donations. The foundation directors believe that all equipment can be recycled. The foundation also sponsors an international program.

Non-Profit Computing, Inc.
40 Wall Street, Suite 2124
New York, NY 10005-1301
To donate computers: 718-357-3416

Non-Profit Computing emphasizes close matching of used computer equipment with not-for-profit organizations and government agencies that can best use the equipment. Non-Profit Computing's client intake process analyzes needs. NPC also offers monthly workshops, computer clinics, and training classes.

Center for Community Computing
P.O. Box 442
Quaker Hill, CT 06375
203-859-1243

The Center for Community Computing consults with not-for-profit organizations regarding their computer needs and offers training. The center provides matching services for donor companies.

Boston Computer Exchange
P.O. Box 1177
Boston, MA 02103
617-542-4414
800-262-6399

The Boston Computer Exchange maintains a substantial list of organizations that want to receive donated computers.

USER GROUPS

Boston Computer Society
One Center Plaza
Boston, MA 02108
617-367-8080

The world's largest personal computer user group is glad to furnish advice about starting up a user group. On an informal basis, they often point callers to existing user groups.

LIQUIDATORS

Computer Hotline
Link House Publications, Inc.
15400 Knoll Trail, Suite 500
Dallas, TX 75248
800-322-5131

Computer Hotline is available by subscription only, on a weekly or monthly basis ($39 weekly, third class; $15 monthly, third class). The publication provides an extensive listing of liquidators in its classified section.

AUCTIONEERS

National Auctioneers Association
8880 Ballentine Street
Overland Park, KS 66214
913-541-8084

The association maintains a list of members, as well as contact names and addresses of directors of state associations. Call them to find an auctioneer in your area.

NATIONAL BROKERS

Boston Computer Exchange
P.O. Box 1177
Boston, MA 02103
617-542-4414
800-262-6399

BCE maintains a list of other brokers around the world and issues licenses to companies who want to become "Seats" on the Exchange. (See Appendix C.)

INSIDE THE BOSTON COMPUTER EXCHANGE

Throughout this book, you've come across references to the Boston Computer Exchange. Here's a thumbnail sketch of how the Exchange operates.

On any late weekday morning, the frantic trading floor at the Boston Computer Exchange in downtown Boston resembles the New York Stock Exchange as callers try to sell an AT for fast cash, upgrade a Mac SE to a Mac II, replace a PC with a new IBM PS/2, or check out the going prices on the Big Board—the computer world's up-to-the-minute arbiter of used computer prices.

BCE is a placement agency for unwanted computers—it helps people get rid of them, which opens space on their desks for new, more advanced computers. The Exchange also handles trade-in machines from major new computer chains such as NYNEX and Valcom and from manufacturers such as Wang and IBM. We describe a typical transaction on the next page.

In any given hour, hundreds of computers are up for sale at the Exchange, with "asks" and "bids" pouring into the brokers by WATS line, FAX, and electronic mail through CompuServe, MCI Mail, and Delphi. When the price is right, the broker matches a buyer with one of the computers in the Exchange's multimillion-dollar "virtual inventory" (in the database, not on site), charging the seller a broker's fee for handling the sale.

First Day

9:50 A.M. You call the Exchange and inquire about buying a used IBM AT. A broker checks the listings and gives you a range of prices for six units with various options. (If you use the coupon at the back of this book, you can order your own printout of the Exchange listings for half-price.)

10:02 A.M. You decide on a mid-range model at a great price.

10:20 A.M. You wire the funds to an escrow account.

10:30 A.M. The Exchange broker instructs the seller to ship the computer to your address via UPS.

Two days later

11:45 A.M. Your equipment arrives. You set it up and test it— everything is fine.

12:30 P.M. You call the Exchange and report that the equipment has arrived and is in good condition.

Nine months later

9:45 A.M. You've outgrown the computer, and you're ready to sell it. You call the Exchange broker, describe your system, and plunk down $25 for a listing. (If you use the coupon at the back of this book, you plunk down only $12.50 to list your machine.)

12:30 P.M. The broker calls you and tells you where to ship your computer.

1:30 P.M. You call the Exchange to buy your next system. The cycle repeats.

Because markets tend to be regional, BCE sells complete kits to people who want to establish exchanges in their own cities. At the time of this writing, the *Seat on the Exchange* kit has been sold to 125 entrepreneurs in locations around the nation and overseas. Each Seat communicates with the Boston office to place bids and to request large volumes of hardware and unusual systems.

Exchange brokers also help buyers and sellers by offering an escrow service. Buyers send funds to the Exchange for clearance through the escrow account, and then the seller ships the equipment to the buyer, who has 48 hours to test the equipment. After the equipment passes the buyer's test, the Exchange releases the buyer's funds to the seller minus a commission. The escrow system is a safe way for strangers to do business over long distances.

The Exchange's weekly *BoCoEx Index: Closing Prices Report* is the acknowledged industry barometer of used computer prices. It keeps the industry apprised of current trends, the hot sellers, and the "dogs" and is carried by *PC Week*, *Computerworld*, CompuServe, Delphi, American CitiNet, and the UPI wire service. Federal government agencies such as the Bureau of Labor Statistics and the Internal Revenue Service also use the index. Use the coupon at the back of this book to order a printed copy of the most recent week's *BoCoEx Index* for half-price—only $2.50.

The range of potential users of the Exchange grows every year, from private individuals and entrepreneurs to multinational corporations and even budding businesses in Eastern Europe.

APPENDIX D

TIPS FOR RETAIL COMPUTER STORES

You are losing sales. Your clients want to buy new computers, but they already own computers. What should they do with them?

You usually mumble something about placing an ad in the local newspaper, and as the client leaves, you hope he or she will figure out something to do with the old computer and come back to buy a new machine from you.

In the early days of the computer business, every buyer was a first-time buyer, and sales were easy. Now the equipment your clients already own is an impediment to their buying new computers. Your profits depend on your ability to help clients sell what they already own.

The situation isn't going to reverse itself—ever. In the 1990s, computer retailers will sell into a replacement market.

As corporations struggle with the problem of what to do with their old equipment, most retail computer stores have yet to address themselves to the trade-in needs of their largest volume new equipment buyers. Computer retailers set up to handle trade-ins have a clear advantage over their competitors who don't. They have tapped into a huge opportunity for the resale of equipment in both volume lots and single sales. And they provide a service to corporate microcomputer managers that brings in corporate customers.

Succeeding at computer sales in the 1990s means providing a channel for equipment to move out of customers' offices so that your new machines can move into their offices. As the obsolescence cycle shortens, helping customers move their old machines will no longer be a "nice touch"—it will be a key to making sales. In the 1990s, you must come to terms with the secondary market:

- Take trade-ins and open a facility to resell used gear. It can be a shelf in the store, a separate store, or a "bargain basement" arrangement. You can take a smaller profit on the sale of new machines and sell the used equipment to get a full measure of profit.

- Send an expert out to the customer's site to recommend ways their machines can be redeployed within the company. Sure, you might lose some immediate sales, but that's short-term, blockhead thinking. If you take a long-term view, you'll realize that the machines you redeploy will eventually come your way as they're shuffled to the bottom. Once you become a corporation's resource for recycling their bottom-tier machines, you'll establish an endless loop of new machines through the front door and used machines out the back door. You'll become an integral part of the company's microcomputer growth plans.

- Advise your corporate customers on the merits of selling vs. donating their used computers. Be prepared to discuss the pros and cons of both options with them. Assess the value of their used machines, and lay out the options for them—sale proceeds vs. tax breaks.

- Put customers directly in touch with local or national services (brokers, liquidators, donation clearinghouses) that can resell or use their existing computers.

- At the very least, recommend this book to your customers. They'll find it as enjoyable, lively, and practical as we think you have.

When you are ready to provide this key service to your customers—help with the disposition of their used computers—put a policy statement together and distribute it to your salespeople and your customers. Make it known that your interest in yesterday's technology is more than an afterthought—it's a key reason to do business with your store today, tomorrow, and well into the future.

INDEX

Dr. Alexander Randall 5th

Alex Randall cofounded the Boston Computer Exchange in 1982. Before that he was a university lecturer, platform speaker, newsletter editor, and thespian. As an American Participant for the US Information Agency and as a lecturer and teacher, he has spoken about computer technology in more than 40 countries all over the world. He is currently featured on the nationally televised program PCTV.

Randall received a bachelor's degree from Princeton University and earned two master's degrees, one in educational technology and the other in international development, from Columbia University. He also earned a doctorate in general systems research at Columbia, where he was a Fellow.

Randall lives on Beacon Hill in Boston with his wife and son and Harris Tweed, their Border collie.

Steven J. Bennett

Steve Bennett is the author of 27 business and computer books. Formerly the president of a technical advertising agency that specialized in biomedicine, he is now executive director of the Bennett Information Group, a research and publishing consortium.

Bennett received a bachelor's degree in psychology and comparative literature from the University of Rochester and a master's degree in regional studies from Harvard University.

He lives in Cambridge, Massachusetts, with his wife and son.